TORDAN

JENNIFER JULIE MILLER

ACKNOWLEDGMENTS

I want to dedicate this book to my husband **Rick.** There are no words to describe my love for you, but the one thing I really want to say is, thank you, for WANTING me, and for being my HERO!

Also, I want to say thanks to my parents, my amazing kids, my beautiful grandkids, my crazy aunt, and all my friends for all your constant support. I want to thank my family for all the hours you have had to listen to the insane ideas inside my head. Even though most of you think I need to be evaluated.

Jennifer Julie Miller

This book is a work of fiction. The names, characters, places, and incidents are the products of the writer's imagination. Any resemblance to actual persons, living or dead, business establishments, events, or locales is entirely coincidental.

COVER ART BY © CREATIVE
COVER DESIGNS (VICKI ADRIAN)
ARTIST

Beta Readers:

Lorene Palmer, Rick Miller, Ethel Nance.

Editors: Partners in Crime Book Services, Randy Henry

Photographs:

Brittany Henry & Rick Miller

CHAPTER 1

LUNA

I swear, it's hotter than the depths of Hell today. I stop long enough to take the rag out of my back pocket so that I can wipe the sweat running down my forehead. I have only been out here a few hours, but the heat is bothering me more than usual. My clothes are nasty and soaked through, everything I have on is clinging to my skin so tightly that I feel like I'm suffocating. I shove my hand down the back of my jeans shoving my panties back down trying to get them unstuck from places they shouldn't be and think to myself, *Damn this sucks.*

What I wouldn't do for a nice breeze about now. Lord knows I'm craving a shower and a cold glass of iced tea, but the sad part is, …any relief, from this heat, is still hours away. I stretch my arms out, shaking my hands as every joint in my body throbs from the strain of swinging this sickle. When I was younger, I didn't notice the long days like I do now, age sucks.

When Dad finally yells for everyone to take a break, I sigh wearily, especially when I look around at what's still left to do. This field is going to take us at least another three more days to finish at this rate, but there is a light at the end of the tunnel... Thank God...,this is the last one we have to finish this year.

It has taken ten of us, mostly friends and neighbors who volunteered to help, working nonstop for the last couple of weeks to cut and hang the tobacco. I don't know what we would have done if they hadn't shown up. There was no way dad, and I could have gotten the fields done alone before they started rotting.

Hopefully, this year's harvest will rate high enough that we can pay off the bank loan and Dad can breathe a little. But I have told myself that for the last three years it seems. No matter what we do we seem to fall short on the money needed to keep us afloat. Now with momma sick. I know my dreams of going to art school will never happen. Dad needs me here helping with the farm more now than ever.

Overwhelmed, I look around at the things that need updating and fixed. Some nights, I sit up late pondering the never-ending list of things we need to do and wonder how Dad still manages to smile with such a heavy load on his shoulders. A lone tear flows down my cheek because no matter how or what I do to help, dad needs more than me. I brush the tears away before Dad sees them and hop up on the wagon. The poor tractor seems as tired as the rest of us as it grumbles when he starts it up. Once everyone is loaded onto the wagon, Dad drives us to one of the big shade trees on the edge of the field where we had dropped the coolers off earlier. I jump off the back only to remember that I had forgotten the chips at the house.

"Dad, I'll be back in a minute, I need to run up to the house and grab the chips."

"Check on your mom while you are there. Take the tractor, it will be quicker."

"I will kiss mom on the cheek for you… and just shut the tractor off. I don't want to tear the yard up with that wagon on the back, it won't turn for shit. I'll only be a minute. You guys go ahead and start without me. There is a roast beef sandwich for you in the gray cooler with your name on it."

"Always taking care of your Daddy, ain't ya, Punkin?"

"Hey, they don't call me Daddy's girl for nothing." I kiss him on the cheek and walk off toward the house. I'm about halfway there when the hairs on the back of my neck stand up, my whole-body tingling in warning. I turn around, wondering if someone has snuck up behind me, only to see them all going through the coolers under the tree.

I rub the back of my neck wearily and turn back around, shoving the feeling off as this damn heat messing with me. I'm only a few feet from the house when it happens again, and this time I know something is wrong. I stop and look up as the air around me… suddenly… feels charged,… like it does moments before lightning strikes the ground, but there's not a cloud in sight. Taking a few more steps I jerk when I swear, I feel someone touching my shoulder. I put my hand up over my nose because of the weird smell in the air. A sudden dizzy spell hits me and my head starts to get fuzzy.

I can hear someone yelling out my name, but it seems so far away. My inner voice tells me to run, that I'm in danger. I stumble a few more steps when I try to turn back towards everyone wondering… *'Am I having a heat stroke?'*

Dad is screaming as he runs towards me. *That's weird, I didn't know Dad could run.* I reach up slowly rubbing my eyes, and yep… Dad still looks like he's running, but he isn't getting any closer. My mind is so dazed it takes me a second to realize he is pointing frantically at something behind me.

I see movement out of the corner of my eye, and I sluggishly look up. The weird smell suddenly gets stronger, and I sway on my feet, simply staring at the thing standing over me. For some reason, …I can't scream, I can't move, and my mind doesn't even react. I'm unnaturally calm. Whatever this is, it's blue, like really dark blue, and is standing above me a good three feet.… Bright orange eyes look me up and down and before I can blink, I'm grabbed from behind by what feels like four massive hands… Hands that are gripping my sides painfully as I'm being pulled away and strangely up.

As I feel my body leaving the ground. I reach out for Dad. He is only a few inches from me now. The last thing I hear before the darkness takes me… is him screaming, "NOOOO!"

CHAPTER 2

LUNA

I wake up screaming… as my back is slammed hard against a cold metal surface. I open my eyes only to shut them back quickly as the pain from the powerful lights above make me feel like they are going to explode inside their sockets. My whole body is spazzing like my nerves are all coming back online at once. It takes everything I have not to scream out from the intensity of the tingling under my skin. After what feels like forever, I start to settle down and I finally have the energy to open my eyes again, squinting as they adjust to the lights. I frown at the oddness of my surroundings.

When I try to raise my head up, I realize I'm being held down by something. I've been strapped down to some sort of hard table. Immediately, I start to jerk my arms and legs against the restraints only to feel my skin tear under the straps like it's made out of paper. The pain makes me whimper and even though I'm at the point of flipping out, I make myself take a few deep breaths and quit pulling against the straps. Mentally, I search my body for any other injuries, but besides my skin, and the fact that my heart is beating so hard it feels like it's going to burst right out of my chest, nothing seems to be bothering me, except I feel sore all over. Like I have been laying around for a long time.

I push the pain away as I try to figure out what's going on. My eyes scan my surroundings, but nothing looks familiar. *Where in the Sam Hell am I?*

A cool breeze floats over me and I start shivering so violently my teeth are chattering. It doesn't take a rocket scientist to realize once I felt the cold air flowing across every inch of my skin that I am naked too. *How in the depths of Hell did I get here, and where is here?*

My mind, is still fuzzy and all I can remember… is reaching out… to someone…but who?

The sound of people crying out has me turning my head. When I register what I'm seeing, I suddenly wish I were still wrapped up in my own mind. There are beds as far as I can see, lined along what appears to be a long hallway. I have to bite the inside of my jaw to keep from screaming when I see another girl being slammed onto the bed next to mine. She no longer hits the table than straps wrap around her body, tying her down, just as I am. It's not even the sight of her being manhandled that terrifies me, nor the fact that she is as naked as I am. It's the blue, four-armed creature who put her there. My mind can't fathom a name for the monstrosities, there is nothing I can compare these life snatchers to... so they are simply... ITs.

My mind clears the moment I see IT! That thing is what snatched me practically out of my dad's arms. It has no humanistic features at all, besides the fact that it's standing on two legs and has a torso. Now, *I don't believe in aliens.* The movies are cool... but we all know that shit ain't real. *Well Einstein, just what the fuck is that then?* I really should stop arguing with myself and just admit that seeing is believing. That's an alien...

An easy nine-foot, four-armed, smurf-colored alien... Its blue arms are so massive I have no idea how it's torso is holding them all up, especially since they are larger than my waist. It's... dark blue skin seems almost leathery in texture, like one of those stretch dolls we all had as kids. Even though it... has a huge body there is no real muscle definition on its huge frame, it's just a blue blob. It has piercings in its pointed ears, large orange eyes, and sunken cheeks seem to dominate its smooshed-up face. Even though I can't be one hundred percent sure, I believe the small piece of material wrapped around its hips is hiding its junk from the world. The blue beast has to be a male, because surely no God would be cruel enough to make any female that damn ugly.

I can hear my dad's words. *'When you are in a situation you can't control, pay attention to what's around you. Don't be a victim...you are a Porter, and we never stop fighting.'* So, I make myself look away from the monsters that are walking in and out of the room and start looking around. Things are hanging from the ceiling that look like metal robotic arms. Some of the beds even have bags full of colored fluids hanging above them. The only other thing I notice are the clear screens that seem to be free floating above each bed…they have flashing symbols dancing across them. At first glimpse, you would think you were in a hospital ward of some kind. Because everything is white and gray, and it smells like anti-septic and blood.

Once I start focusing on my surroundings, I notice a slight vibration under the curved table I'm on. So, we have to be on some sort of ship or vessel. I'm thinking total *Star Trek* here… as I'm still in denial at what my eyes are processing. I have never been a huge Sci-Fi girl. I mean we have all heard of Area Fifty-One our whole lives, but who believes in that crap? Apparently, I do… now… because there is no denying it: …the damn things that are packing human girls in here and throwing them on the beds next to mine… are full-blown aliens.

The blue things just keep coming in and out. Packing girls either over their shoulders like a sack of potatoes or dragging them behind on the floor, completely ignoring their screams of pain.

Either they had this planned, or they have been doing this for a long time, because they are way too organized. Even the beds look like they were designed to hold something our size. I look back down the row of girls, there have to be at least twenty or more of us here. Apparently, they have abducted every and any age too, as I can see older women mixed in with some that have to be in high school.

ALIENS. No matter how many times I repeat it in my head, it's just not registering…. I mean, now come on, if aliens were snatching girls from all over the world, wouldn't the governments know it? Don't we have radars, satellites, and crap that would see the Grabbers of Doom entering our atmosphere?

Everyone on Earth has to be in a panic right now. I know my dad…he will never stop, but… what can one man do if the rest of the world turns a blind eye to the disappearances? They will say he is crazy…that he made all of it up…I can't let myself dwell on the what IFs…all I can do is hope. Because, surely, they are trying to find a way to get us back. …I know people come up missing every day, but not this many at once. Someone else had to see at least one of us being taken. Rationalizing this all in my mind is the only thing keeping me from breaking down into full-blown panic mode.

I pull on the restraints again, refusing to believe there is no way out of here. The more I tug on the straps the madder I get. I will not let my mind crumble; I'm terrified, but I will be damned if I let them know it.

The majority of the girls are crying or screaming hysterically… only a few are fighting against their restraints. One of the blue beasts slams a hand down on one of the girls struggling, yelling something at her like he wants her to stop. What do those stupid fuckers think we're going to do? Just lay here and hope for the best? There isn't a female alive that knows when you're restrained naked, you're in deep shit. But when I see one of them fondling the girl next to me as she struggles to get away from it, I yell out.

"Get your nasty ass paws off her, you pervert! Let me guess, the only way you can get it up is if we're helpless, right? Let me the fuck out of these straps and let's see how well you do when we fight back, you ugly fucker."

He turns towards me when he hears my voice. Snarling, I can see his blackened, rotted teeth as he makes these weird clicking noises.

"Fucking body snatching scum. Only worthless pieces of shit like you would take another from their families and lives. Let me guess, your little blue peckers won't get up if a female comes willingly."

I should have known things were only going to get worse when he looks past me and smiles, or I think that was supposed to be a smile. Something grabs me by my neck, slamming me hard against the table. This time, I don't even try to hold back the scream because the thing that just grabbed me is terrifying, something only a nightmare could create. Bright yellow and green skin patches are stretched tightly over all its muscles, making it look completely deformed and repulsive.

The yellow nightmare… loosens its hold on me for a second, enough at least for me to be able to speak, …and before I can stop myself, I say, "Damn, you have a face only a mother could love, you put the F in fucking ugly, buddy."

It growls down at me, large canine-shaped teeth dripping saliva upon my chest as its black eyes sparkle maliciously. Long, skinny fingers tipped with black claws start sliding up and down my sides. I try to jerk away only for one of the blue assholes to grab my ankles. I whimper, as its claws cut into my skin lightly all the way from my shoulders to the top of my legs. The cuts are so deep that I feel like my skin is being shredded into small pieces. I bite my cheek to keep from screaming out, but I never stop fighting the restraints. If this yellow nightmare thinks I'm simply going to lay here and take this, it's highly mistaken.

Nightmare… pushes down on my neck harder, and I start to see black spots in front of my eyes. I'm so focused on trying to breathe that I miss it moving its other hand up my torso, gripping the tender flesh of my breast and when it sinks its claws in deep, I can't hold back the scream as my body arches off the table from the pain.

It lets go of me completely and I gasp for air, only to watch the yellow nightmare's face lower towards my breast. Its jaws unhinging wide, …snake-like, and before I can move, it strikes, biting a huge hunk out of the side of my breast. I cry out in agony, watching through tear-filled eyes as it chews on my flesh like I'm a piece of rare steak.

Nightmare… smiles over at the blue beast right before he swallows the meat of my breast. I have no idea what comes out of my mouth after that. It's like something snapped deep inside of me. But, I know, I call it every vulgar name stored in my vocabulary. This, unfortunately, only seems to amuse it more, and once again before I can react, it runs black claws across my stomach, but this time the cuts are deep. I yell out again, panting against the pain radiating through my body as it amuses itself as it slowly tortures me.

Nightmare… plays in the blood pooling around my cuts like it's painting a picture on my skin that isn't marred yet. smearing blood all over my stomach and down the tops of my legs like it's some sort of salad dressing. When its long fingers scrape across my clit, I squeeze my legs together as tightly as I can. If Nightmare thinks I'm just going to lay here while it rapes me it's going to be mistaken. My dad didn't raise a quitter and I will fight… until my very last breath.

The blue beast forces my legs apart and I cry out as the yellow nightmare takes a huge bite out of the inside of my thigh. I gag this time at the sound it's making as it chews on my flesh. My whole body is quivering in pain at this point. I fight unconsciousness, only to feel it insert one of those long-clawed fingers into my tender folds, shredding my insides as it moves its claws in and out of me. Tears run down my cheeks as the pain takes over my mind. *Why is this happening to me? What choices in my life did I make to lead me to this moment? What have I done that was so bad God has allowed me to be punished so?*

Finally, Nightmare removes its blade-like finger from inside of me, and I watch as it licks the blood off its claws. The yellow human flesh eater …brings its face down towards mine like it's interested in my reaction to the pain they're causing me. I spit in its face. My mind slowly splinters as I laugh hysterically at Nightmare's reaction…it jerks back, wiping its face off like I'm the sicko here.

The yellow destroyer yells at me, grabbing me roughly as it shakes me all over. Hands tear into my flesh as I feebly try to squirm away. When I don't act or reply to what Nightmare is saying,… apparently this pisses it off… *Go figure.* Because the look on its face changes from enjoyable torture… to rage.

Nightmare grabs my face with its long claws, sinking them forcefully into the skin on my cheeks as it tries to pry my lips apart. At this point, there isn't much fight left in me, but I still try. Unfortunately, its strength overcomes mine easily, and as it inserts its fingers into my mouth, I take the last bit of strength I have left and bite down hard, happy to feel at least one of them crush under my teeth.

Instead of Nightmare pulling back as I had hoped, it starts to make a sound like it's laughing, forcing its hand farther back into my mouth where my teeth are no longer a threat. Before I can comprehend what it's doing. I feel its other hand grab my bottom jaw, ripping my cheeks apart, tearing them all the way to my ears. The bones snap apart as my jaw hangs loosely, the only thing holding the lower part of my face on is the skin still attached below my ears.

And when I think it can't get any worse, Nightmare grabs the end of my tongue, ripping it from my mouth. I start convulsing, drowning as I gag upon my own blood. My mind starts shutting down, no longer able to deal with the agony, or the horrors inflicted upon my body. Suddenly, I'm tossed onto the floor.

I can hear Nightmare screaming at me again as I lay here, but I don't have the strength to move. The fight to breathe is the only response I have now since my blood is choking me. I feel my ribs burst within my chest when something kicks me in the side, and I go flying across the room. Welcoming the feeling of nothingness when I hit a wall hard. Especially, when the pain just stops… now that my head is too heavy to hold up. I know I'm only seconds from death.

My very last thoughts are, *Daddy, would have been proud of me, I never stopped fighting.*

CHAPTER 3

LUNA

I can hear a voice in the distance, "Human, it is time to awaken."

"Master ENAC, I have given the command for the female to awaken, but there is still no brain activity."

"AMI, administer a light shock to her system, we have not come this far for this experiment to fail."

The pain… starts mildly at my feet, slowly making its way up my body with a light tingle, only to get stronger the farther up it travels. By the time it makes it to my chest, my whole body is arching unnaturally upwards. I try to reach out, only to find I'm surrounded by nothingness. The smell of fumes makes me want to cough, but my mouth won't open. Reaching up, I claw at the bottom of my face only for my hands to be grabbed and restrained. My body feels suspended like I'm floating in the air instead of being on a solid surface.

"Calm yourself, female, you have no reason to panic. Let your senses open up to your surroundings and breathe out of your nose. I'm going to settle your form onto the operating table, and I want you to sit up and remain calm. That is a direct order."

I immediately stop fighting against the cold fingers holding me. Slowly, my eyes come into focus, and I jerk back when a single eyeball darts in front of my face. When the blurriness finally recedes, I see a room with flashing lights and multiple arms working in tandem on what looks like me. I blink my eyes again trying to focus on what I'm seeing, then it all disappears. I shake my head, confused.

"Master ENAC, brain function is slowly coming back online. The female's flesh seems to be reacting properly to stimulation. Her eye stems are adjusting well but need to be reset. I'm showing an unnatural spike in her brain waves as she is recalling some of the recorded procedures in modifying her system."

I can hear voices around me, but who is this female they are talking about? The fingers on my left hand are throbbing and I slowly look down only to see what I think are fingers laying on my lap. I raise my arm only to be horrified that those metal fingers are connected to my own wrist. I turn my hand back and forth in front of my eyes. When the metal fingers stretch out, I realize... I did that without thinking.

I lift my right arm up and even though it seems to have marks and bruises all over the flesh it looks normal. I bring both hands up in front of my face, mimicking all my movements with each hand. If I hadn't seen it with my own eyes, I would have never known the left hand wasn't mine as it responds to my every thought.

"Female, can you shake your head in confirmation that you can hear me?"

Something speaking to me has me striking out, the eye moves quickly out of the way as I jerk, looking around for the voice that is suddenly in my head. My eyes start to blur in and out as I begin to shake all over. I start to open my mouth to ask what's happening to me, only to realize no sound comes out. When I reach my hand up I only feel smooth metal under my fingertips. I start hyperventilating, then something is jabbed into the side of my neck. I fall backward, darkness taking me once again.

"Master ENAC, I had to administer a sedative. The subject is reacting poorly to the enclosure we secured to the bottom of her face. I believe some minor adjustments need to be made before we reanimate her again. The female's interface we placed inside of her brain seems to be functioning properly, but we may need to plant some false information in her brain, as she awoke in a puzzled state."

"AMI, program the female to believe she has always been part machine. She will have a greater chance of succeeding if she believes this is her normal state. See if prior memories can be erased or blocked. Then give her a name and new memories quickly before her body starts to reject the parts we have installed. I have a few buyers ready to purchase this unit if she remains stable. If she starts to deteriorate, she can be put with the others, out in the fields."

"Yes, Master ENAC."

CHAPTER 4

TORDAN

"Falcor, acknowledge my landing on Targres Four. I will disconnect all transmissions until I clear intake into sector two."

"Acknowledged."

I head to my personal quarters on the shuttle to gather the few items I'm taking with me. Targres Four is divided into four extremely different sectors. All of them are controlled by different types of factors. Gangs, dirty politicians, and sentient AI's… are just a couple of things I will have to watch out for as I try to integrate myself into their system. After debating many scenarios with DaR, SoL, and XuL during the last few rotations… this was the only solution we could come up with for this mission.

My main focus is the scientific farm-based sector. From the planet scans we have been able to study we believe this is where the female human is being held. There are massive fields surrounding the main compound, but we can't get our scanners past the main Guard bots.

One of the few things we do know is… that these specific scientists believe they are above any and all laws. They are not even trying to control the rumors of a rogue AI who is stealing corpses or anything organic to experiment on. Of course, because all I have are rumors to go on, I have to tread quietly until I have some hard evidence. Apparently, no one alive has actually seen anything that can be used to shut this facility down. It's one of those cases where everyone knows what's going on, but no one wants to act on it. If they are simply growing and selling produce and other grown goods, why do they need so many guards?

One of the many rumors is that the AI is even paying the prostitutes at one of the local Hostel houses drugs to bring in any species they can. It's harvesting any and all organic parts… and paying well if the rumors are correct. From my understanding, it's looking for a way to merge itself into a living host. Falcor and SCOUT have been monitoring the area secretly for some time now, especially after we were notified that there may be a human female there, but recently they lost all feeds. I know I'm not going to be able to simply stroll in there and demand that they hand her over if there is one.

The second sector is the pleasure center of the planet, it's known for its many brothels and drinking establishments. What it doesn't advertise is it's also a place where you can purchase exotic slaves at an underground market, and where thieves run free with little or no laws to stop them.

The third, shocking enough, is a major vacation area. Its pink sand beaches and the private suites that are offered to couples only are huge with the newly mated. What most don't know …is that over a third of the couples who come here to celebrate their new union come up missing, never to be heard from again. That is why when SoL brought Alana here earlier in the Lunar Rotation, I demanded he stay connected to me or Falcor at all times. Alana swears she saw a human female in one of the outer fields, and because we can't scan the entire planet, I made the decision to investigate it myself. Especially now with the destruction of Earth, human females will become an even hotter commodity and DaR also swore to Kira he would have every rumor investigated. So, here I am, as we all feel like it's our duty to save as many of the females as possible.

I have a slightly more personal reason for coming, even though I have never spoken this out loud. The idea of having a female of my very own has proven to be a major distraction in my every rising routine. A mate is something I honestly didn't know I was missing until the discovery of the human females. I have started to envy my best friend and that's unacceptable.

There are only two main ports in and out of Targres. Because I don't want to be detected, I cloak my smaller personal shuttle as I enter its atmosphere and land it in the fourth sector unauthorized. This sector is desolate… Nothing can grow or live out here long without major resources. The heat of one single rotation would kill most and it's not the only deadly thing out in this region.

"Falcor, I need you to monitor the shuttle and ignite the cooling tanks if the temperatures start to interfere with the sensors. I'm also setting parameter sensors to notify you if anyone tries to board or mess with the shuttle."

"Confirmed."

I shake my head and smile, because of Falcor's one-word answers. He is more advanced than ANDI, SAGE, or SCOUT combined, but he still refrains from forming any personal traits, or attachments. I wonder what it's going to take to shake the big guy up.

Walking out of the shuttle, I hit the control panel to double-check the cloaking device. The ship will become invisible to the naked eye and undetectable on the radar unless someone actually bumps into it. The shuttle will only re-emerge with my touch or the sound of my voice. I haven't taken more than a few steps when I have to stop and I pull my long cape up and over my head. The heat is so intense I feel like my exposed skin is already blistering. I stop long enough to consider where to start my search.

This is one of the few moons or planets I have ever been on that the sky and the ground are practically the same color depending on where you're located. There are shuttles and ships flying overhead in and out of the two major ports. A few of the buildings are so large that they actually block the rays of the two suns that are the center of this side of the galaxy. I walk through the busy streets looking for a place to hole up until I figure out how to make some connections.

One thing is always the same no matter where you are. If you need information, you have to loosen their tongues. So, with that in mind, I head to the nearest drinking establishment.

I walk into the End of the Universe bar and entertainment. The voices quiet down at my sudden appearance through the door and every eye turns my way. I access my surroundings immediately, looking out over the diverse crowd in this establishment. When I don't see any real threats, I pull my hood off, strolling up to the long bar that stretches all the way across the room. The cool air feels wonderful after walking through the intense heat of sector four to get here. I was momentarily shocked to see a small Valerian male wiping down the counter.

"What can I provide for you this rising?"

"Brytos."

I watch the Valerian male pour the beverage out of an ancient machine as I scan the crowd.

He sets the drink down in front of me and I know my cybernetic eye glows bright orange as I look into the glass, verifying there is nothing harmful in its contents.

"General, only a foolish male would bring on the wrath of Darverius by drugging your drink. What business brings you to this part of the galaxy?"

"I see you know who I am… That is disappointing, but if anyone asks,… I'm on leave." He simply nods his head yes. "I believe this is the first time I have ever seen one from your world in such a place. I would think so many auras would be overwhelming for you. Especially serving drinks in such a lovely establishment?"

"For most of my kind, yes, but I have built a tolerance for such things. I know you seek something. I can feel it. Unfortunately, I have dampened my senses to the point that I can no longer devise what it is you are looking for. But as always, I know more than I should. Is there possibly a place of leisure I can point you to? A place more befitting your status, with better company?"

"You would do better not to involve yourself."

"Appreciated, but unnecessary. If you are seeking information, you won't find it here, or anywhere in this sector. People who gossip tend to disappear rather quickly. Watch where you voice your questions or where you receive your answers. There are ears and eyes everywhere."

"Where would you suggest?" He doesn't say another word, simply walks off to attend to others. Species of every sort come in and out of the drinking establishment as I enjoy my beverage. The Valerian male handles the many orders being called out at him, calmly going from one thing to the next. I no longer set my empty container down, that he fills it again. He looks straight at me and then looks up without moving his head.

I turn slowly, with drink in hand, casually leaning back against the bar. Lifting my head up, I take a drink to see what he is trying to show me. There is a large round viewing monitor attached to the ceiling. These are common sights in most establishments, but I can see the hidden cameras behind its reflective surface… most wouldn't. I finish my drink sitting it back on the counter only to put my hand over the top when he starts to fill it again.

"I suggest you head back to Falcor, General. This planet is not kind to strangers, especially ones who travel alone."

"I appreciate your warning and will take it into consideration. Thank you for your service." I don't wait for a reply, I simply scan my currency chip and walk back out. I'm several leagues away from the establishment before I comm DaR on our private channel.

"DaR."

"Yes, Tordan."

"I made contact with a local and it is confirmed that many come up missing, especially if alone. There are security bots posted throughout the region, but I have not been approached by one yet.

"I plan on finding lodging this darkness and, with first light, I will proceed with our plan. So far, I have seen nothing out of order, besides the extensive security posted around the border of sector one."

"Tordan, I still believe it was an error to send you in alone. I know we all discussed this mission at length, but I have a bad feeling about this. So, as Kira would say, *just in case,*' I had Falcor instruct EvO to move Devastation into Targres Four's planetary rotation. He was notified to cloak the ship against their detection and to await further instructions. If we lose contact, I will send his battle legion planet side immediately to retrieve you."

"This was not the original plan, DaR."

"No, but it is now. If you find one of the remaining females do not engage until you have backup. That planet has perfected its way of covering up its disappearances and I don't want your name added to the list."

"Confirmed."

"Tordan, that was a direct order."

"I heard you, DaR."

"I don't like that tone."

"I have no tone… you're in my head… it's not like I'm speaking to you directly." All of a sudden, a squealing noise blares inside of my head. "DaR, DaR?" A whispering voice interrupts the private comm unit I have with DaR.

"Please stop talking…You must be quiet; they can hear you."

"DaR, did you hear that?"

"We have been compromised. I want you to return to your shuttle immediately, Tordan. Tordan!"

As much as it is against my training, I block his incoming command, more now determined than ever.

CHAPTER 5

LUNA

Startled, I stop to look around. Somehow, I have picked up odd voices on my inner communication device. The tone of one of the male's voices sends tingles throughout my system as the dark raspy sound comes in and out...Broken words and partial sentences are all I can make out as he speaks to someone called DaR.

When I see one of the security bots turn my way, I immediately bend back down and start picking the small beans off the plant in front of me. This isn't the first time I have heard another's voice in my head that wasn't AMI, or Master ENAC...but it's the first time I wanted to see the face that went with it.

That thought no more hits my sensors than I shut it down. I learned years ago to stop wanting anything. My sole purpose is to assist AMI and to work in the outer fields where the crops have to be handpicked because machinery will destroy the valuable crop.

I'm the oldest remaining test subject still alive here. Most only make it a few seasons before their bodies start to shut down. I have just recently started to deteriorate even with the advanced serum AMI is currently providing me with. The few of us that have survived learned to talk back and forth on untraceable channels, but this male is practically screaming,… *here I am*. That's when it dawns on me… if I can hear him, it's possible the others can too. I raise my eyes, glancing around the field. None of the others seem to be acting any differently.

I speak straight to the stranger before I think it through. *"Please stop talking…You must be quiet. They can hear you…run…escape this place while you can."*

The moment I connect with him, I grab my head in pain as his sensory projector tries to latch onto mine. It takes me a moment, but I'm able to block him from being able to trace me. Normally, I'm not this foolish and if AMI runs a diagnosis on me this darkness, she will ask me about the abnormal log. I will have no other option than to tell her the truth. I try to stay out of the way and unnoticed as ENAC will use any reason to dispose of me now that my deterioration has started. We are not worth maintaining if we are not at a hundred percent working capacity. He reminds me constantly about the money he has lost on me.

The second I speak through the open channel I notice Hugo, the only other sentient cyborg still functioning, looking over at me.

He must have heard me. *Frack.* Hugo is a huge red male Phogx with dark symbols burned onto his skin and face. At one time I believe he was someone of importance, but he was destroyed in his prime. One of ENAC's many harvesters found him after a battle on a planet called Darverius. Because he was presumed dead, no one ever looked for his body. That's how ENAC has escaped detection all this time, he only takes the ones that are supposed to be deceased, or undocumented.

At first, I often helped AMI with new patients, or organics as we're called. I don't know who was more shocked, AMI or me, when the male Phogx opened his eyes and called me a Human. He said that I was rare... and that he had been but moments from obtaining one of his own when she appeared unmarked in a public marketplace. AMI immediately reset the unit when I questioned her about it. She told me that the programming she had just inserted was faulty, but I didn't and I still don't believe her. Because the new patient hadn't had the memory dampeners inserted yet. He knew what I was... before. That was the first time I questioned my existence.

I asked Hugo about it again later on, but of course, he didn't remember any of it afterwards. Once the dampeners are working properly you can barely remember your last rising. Mine have never worked fully. There are times especially when I'm in rest mode when I will dream of another life. Where different faces and voices talk to me in the darkness. Unfortunately, I always wake back up in the same small chamber and the dreams fade no matter how hard I try to hold onto them.

This rising is no different. AMI sends out a signal and we all awaken at the same time. Once dressed, we meet in the substance room. Hugo and I are the only ones who need hard substances to survive. The others simply plug in. I proceed to the replicator and instruct the machine to create my usual. A ground up mixture of vitamins and proteins my organic body needs to continue to function properly.

Hugo devours his huge plate of food while my feeding tube slowly pulls the soft ingredients into my stomach. As I watch him eat, an image from one of my dreams reemerges for a moment. I see a different version of myself for a second, I'm standing in front of a viewing monitor, swirling material around my legs back and forth… smiling.

I push the image from my mind as I know it has to be fake, something my consciousness has made up. The whole lower part of my face is metal. I have no teeth to smile with or a mouth to eat like Hugo does. An odd sensation settles upon me once again of what I think is sadness. This feeling has plagued me since my creation.

I questioned AMI if she had the same type of feelings…she told me it was natural for one such as me to have an active imagination. That it was part of my programming and what makes me such a good organic is my range of emotion. I have no idea what that was supposed to mean. As I can't openly communicate with anyone but her and Master ENAC. And I'm only allowed to speak to Hugo about the crops or anything related. We both learned that lesson the hard way.

"Luna, when you are through receiving substance, I require your assistance."

I finish quickly and head to the medical room, worried she is going to ask me about the voice I heard last rising. AMI is the room itself. She functions from a single viewer and can operate with multiple extensions at once. Her core system runs various sentient programs at all times, as each of us needs her in a different way.

"Luna, I have a task for you today… a job that is different in nature than you are accustomed to. There is a rare shipment of medical supplies being smuggled into the market in the pleasure sector. I need you to obtain them for me. They are trying to find a way to cut us out of their medical procedures and Master ENAC wants this to be stopped immediately.

"I am sending the instructions and all the information I have about the products to you as we speak. You are not to be compromised or discovered in any way. If you fail and they obtain you, I have been given instructions to terminate you before they can upload your interface for information."

"I will not fail you." I take a deep breath, relieved that she didn't ask me why I warned the strange voice in my head, because I don't know what I would have said. AMI's voice brings me back out of my daydreaming.

"I told the Master those exact words, Luna. This mission is crucial to the Master's plans for you and your survival here depends on your success. Do you understand me?"

I shake my head yes as my eyes flutter, ...assessing the information AMI is sending me. I immediately turn from the room and head towards my own chambers as my mind goes through the multiple strategies and scenarios AMI has shown to me. I pick the one with the highest rate of success and proceed accordingly once I receive my cloak and gloves from my room. I head toward the underground tunnels that no one besides myself, AMI, and Master ENAC are aware of.

Climbing a retractable ladder, I send out a signal connecting myself to all the Guard bots in the area, using their eyes as my own. When I see that the area is clear, I push the panel up and out of the way as I ascend from the tunnel below. Once I replace the panel, I scan the area again for any threats.

I pull my cloak up and over my head, hiding my features and blend into the crowd. When I hear a group of rowdy drinkers approaching, I duck behind a column and wait until they pass by me, then I slide in behind them, using their drunken steps and sounds to mask my presence.

The feeling of someone watching me has me sending feelers out. The Guard bots look around for anything or anyone out of place. When nothing is reported back to me, I cut away from the crowd and make my way to the market. I'm smart enough not to head straight toward the stands that are reported to hold the medicine I'm here to take.

I allow myself a moment of freedom and stop at several stands, admiring the local artists. My hand reaches out involuntarily to a necklace laying on top of one case. The necklace is heart-shaped with odd, clear-like stones wrapped around one side. It's small compared to the other items on the table… invisible in the flashiness around it.

The moment I have it in my hand…a memory flashes in front of me. Once again, I'm in front of a viewing monitor watching the stones sparkle as the sunlight bounces off its many facets. Someone calling my name has me looking back through the viewing monitor…a mirror,… it's called… and before I can see anything else the memory fades.

I understand now… what I'm seeing…. It was simply easier to believe what I was told and to follow my base programming than it was to fight against it. I have been in denial for quite some time. This necklace and the voice I heard last rising have me questioning the things I have been seeing only in my dreams. I don't believe I have always been here. I'm just like the others they have brought in.

I have no way of purchasing this necklace, so I sit it back down. My heart jerks painfully in my chest as it leaves my fingers. I turn away from the temptation and for a moment I forget myself and where I am. My eyes settle on another in a distance, even covered in a cloak there is no hiding the strength of his form and I know immediately this is the owner of that voice.

"You."

The male is looking straight at me, as my eyes settle on his face. I swear I feel my soul call out to him. There is something comforting in his yellow eyes. Before I can say anything to him, the sound of a laser pistol discharging has me ducking down instinctively. The stranger is immediately forgotten as I use this distraction to slide into the stand I have been monitoring.

The occupants are so busy evading the stray laser beams, they pay no attention to my small form slinking into their space. Thanks to AMI's download I know exactly what I'm looking for. I scan the area looking for anything putting off a slight charge as the meds are inside a small cooling device.

The moment I see it, I grab the case and slide out of the back of the enclosure. Hiding the case inside my cloak, I step into the back aisle only to trigger one of the Guard bots. It turns abruptly towards me, ready to fire if I take another step. It takes me precious seconds to send the override codes into its system for it to shut down.

I send another signal out to the remaining Guard bots and quickly make my way back to the access panel. I'm in such a hurry to get back inside the compound, I almost screw up by not scanning the area before opening the panel. The fight in the market couldn't have broken out at a better time as most are running the opposite way. No one wants to be in that area when the Security bots show up. They don't ask questions. They simply retain everyone in the area, guilty or not.

When the scans show that there is no one around, I lift the panel and then climb down the ladder quickly, the panel shutting on its own above me. I send further instructions out to the closest

Guard bot to watch the area until darkness, then it can resume its normal rotation.

I pull my cloak off and drape it over my arm as I hurry toward AMI. I am only steps away when her outer door slides open. "Luna, please place the refrigerant container on the counter and have a seat on the bed."

I sit down, awaiting my next instructions.

"Perfect, it's all here, the container you retrieved has all the vials I was in need of. I notified Master ENAC of your success, and he is very happy with you Luna, as am I. I had no doubts about your success." Before she can finish telling me anything, Master ENAC's voice comes through the room.

"AMI, prepare the subject for repair and reactivate the female's internal reproductive system."

"Master, Luna's uterus is impure. That's why she was considered defective, I'm not sure my systems have the knowledge to reverse such damage as this was genetic to her organic form."

"You are correct AMI, your system cannot repair the endometriosis that has weaved its way throughout her system, but the vials she recovered can and will. The process will be taxing on her weakened system, so you will have to monitor the female at all times.

"I want a pure breed specimen. All of my research indicates the only way I can truly become sentient is through an original blank form. The youngling will be born and immediately placed into a processing vat where my own interface will be merged, giving me full access to its physical form.

"Because of its small, undeveloped form, it will be vulnerable. Without any natural defenses that could purge me from its system, it will be easily manipulated. I will accelerate its growth process and should be fully formed within six Orbital rotations. Once this process starts, I want you to lock down the compound until I'm back in control."

"Master EVEC, what about the other organics and the crops?"

"The crops will be tended to by Worker bots, just as we did before we incorporated the organics. The others will be disposed of."

"What of Luna? Will you keep her alive to nurture the youngling until you are mature enough to feed on your own? The research I have on their forms shows that the youngling has a higher survival rate if fed directly from their biological parent."

"I have not decided at this time what I will do with the incubator."

"Master ENAC, we have one other issue to consider before we go forward. Even if this medication manages to clear her diseased uterus for birth, we have no active sperm to activate her eggs. Hugo is the only other male in residence, and I neutered him right after activation."

"I will have the male source delivered shortly. You will need to prepare a separate med chamber for the incoming species as I will be instructing you to do multiple experiments on him. I knew the moment my sensors picked up his bio reads that it was time to activate the last part of my plan.

"The male's fully-functioning form will finally complete my research. His organic body is fully integrated with his cybernetic enhancements. Once we confirm conception, we will dissect him to study further. I have to know how his maker kept him from deteriorating."

CHAPTER 6
TORDAN

I am walking through the market scanning the beings around me when a flash of something unworldly catches my attention. I step back out of the way of the others who are walking through, only for it to twinkle again.

I look around only to find a small form holding the sparkling object on the other side of the market. As my cybernetic eye zooms in on the item in its hand, I immediately realize the piece is of earthly materials. The wind picks up suddenly and the small form's cloak is pushed back, revealing a flash of silver before it lowers its head back down. I watch it put the piece of jewelry back onto the stand and then fold its hand up into a fist. When it suddenly turns... bright blue eyes lock onto mine.

"You."

I hear her voice… a bare whisper in my head.… My mind immediately recognizes the voice that had interrupted me and DaR earlier. I thought the voice was female but in all of my dreams, I couldn't have imagined the sight in front of me. Her cloak did an excellent job hiding her from the others, but my cybernetics can even see through most metals.

I'm shocked to see that she is human, or at least she is half-human now. The whole lower part of her face has been replaced by metal and I detect other alloys scattered throughout her small frame. Someone has butchered her… used her tiny body as an experiment. My anger rises as I can't focus on anything besides the sad eyes staring back at me. I suddenly want to hold her in my arms… do anything in my power to chase that sadness away.

I start to step toward her only to hear a laser pistol being fired next to me. I drop down instantly as a firefight breaks out around me. Backing out of range my eyes search for the female, but she is gone. I had only taken my eyes off her for a moment, and I have already lost her. I stoop down, running across the market to where she had been only moments before; still, she is nowhere in sight. "Frack." At least now I know the rumors are true, now to locate her again.

Reaching across the stand, I pick up the small piece of jewelry she had in her hand when I first saw her. Still feeling the warmth of her fingers upon it. I scan my currency chip without even asking the merchant for the price, then open the inner panel of my arm up, laying the piece inside for safekeeping.

I start to slip out the back of one of the stalls when I hear DaR yelling out orders. Started by the sound of his voice, I look back down the path I had just come from only to see him and several others pinned down by the laser fire.

I have no idea how he got here this fast or who he's already pissed off, but it looks like I'm going to have to get involved. "DaR, who have you pissed off already? DaR, come in!"

"Tor... u...r...not."

"Frack, something is jamming our signal."

I pull my pistol out, setting it on stun, and fire at the one closest to me. I see the cloaked figure fall back. Then I wave at DaR to advance. I will cover them until he can get to better cover.

To my absolute horror, instead of DaR dodging out of the line of fire, he starts walking right down the center of the aisle. I don't even think about it as I dart in front of him, reaching out to tackle him to the ground only for my arm to pass through his body. I stumble, falling to my knees. DaR's laughter echoes all around me as I'm completely confused about what just happened.

Distracted, I don't move in time as a stray beam catches me. I jerk as I'm hit by the laser fire gripping my side. I grit my teeth as I pull myself out of the way and behind another table. I pull my hand out away from my side only to see it covered in my own blood. "Frack. nothing is going my way today!" Glancing around the table I see DaR being jumped at the same time by three of the goons firing at him.

I know handling three at once is easy for him, but it doesn't feel right, something about the way he is moving is off. When I see one of them hit him in the back and he goes down on one knee, I think, *He has to be hurt badly to go down that easily.* I throw the table out of the way I was crouched behind and barrel into the one who just knocked him down. I hear a laser ready to fire and I turn just in time to roll the guy over in front of me, using his body as a shield.

Then with my foot. I knock the gun out of the other one's hand enjoying hearing the sound of his arm breaking in the process. I throw the guy I just used as a shield to the side and launch myself at the last one. My cybernetic arm practically knocks his head off.

I grab DaR's arm, pulling him up. "Are you injured? I have never seen you go down that easily. We have to get out of here. I can hear the security bots headed this way."

DaR grabs my arm, yelling out... "He is over here!"

"What the Frack?"

DaR's hood falls back and the smile that greets me isn't my friend. The face is similar... and from a distance, or if you didn't know DaR well you would think this was him. But this is not DaR...unfortunately... Even with my knowledge this imposter still fooled me.

"Who are you?"

"Oh, you haven't had the pleasure, have you? It's nice to finally see what the mighty second hand to the powerful commander looks like in the flesh…. Tordan, my new metal friend… thanks for saving my ass back there. Just so you know, I was simply toying with them, hoping you would intervene."

"Who are you?"

"I'm my father's nightmare, his… SiN!"

I try to jerk my arm out of his grip only to realize. I can't move.

"I might be a little more than I appear, or even slightly more than a male wearing my father's pretty face… I'm so happy we have met face to face this rising. I have so many surprises to share with you all, but sadly for you, I have decided not to give away all my secrets today…but…nothing makes me happier than to see my plan advancing…. I understand you are star-struck with the beauty of my face…and because I so enjoy being told I look just like my father….It always puts me in such a good mood… I will let you in on a few things that you will have no power to stop.

"I plan on ruining you… and all that he holds dear…one person at a time. I have intercepted every communication you have had with him while on this planet. He will have no idea until it's too late, that it's not your voice he is hearing in his head… but mine. By the time he realizes something is wrong and comes for you… you will be dead, and he will grieve deeply because he only has himself to blame.

"The best part is…the moment he leaves his precious little female behind to save you. I plan on stepping in and taking her. I just don't know how long I will play with her before I send her head back to him in a box. He will rue the day he was born when I'm finished. I will destroy all he loves, all he has created…all he covets, and when he is on his knees, I will take his life."

I can't help but laugh at the male standing in front of me. "Boy, you are delusional. You are no match for your father. He didn't get where he is this rising by strength alone. You may be lucky enough to win a few rounds, but you don't know your father. And I guarantee you won't win this game you're playing. Your hatred for him is unwarranted. He had no idea you even existed."

The male screams out, **"He does now!"**

A large Security bot approaches, and before I can say anything SiN does. "Take this male into custody, ENAC has a bounty on his head."

"Under whose authority?" the bot asks.

To my horror, I watch SiN slide back the sleeve of his cloak. The mark of the House of DaR is plainly displayed there on his arm.

"Where did you get that?" I finally am able to break his hold on me and I step away flashing the same symbol on my inner arm to the Security bot. "I'm General Tordan, second in command to Falcor, and I demand that you arrest this man, this male is an imposter!"

The Security bot blinks as it goes offline momentarily, when it reboots a net is thrown over me securing me to the ground. SiN smiles as I struggle to free myself of this net. "You have no idea what I'm capable of. I hope you enjoy the rest of your stay here on this lovely planet."

All I can hear is his laughter as he walks away when the Security bot says. "Sector two appreciates your assistance with obtaining this criminal, Commander DaR."

Before I can say another word, something jabbing me from behind has me falling to my knees. My whole-body spazzes as the darkness takes me.

CHAPTER 7

DAR

"Tordan come in?.. Frack!"

A small delicate hand being placed upon my arm stops my pacing. "What's wrong DaR?"

"I can't get Tordan to answer me. I've had a bad feeling about this mission from the moment he left. I could have sworn he just tried to talk to me, but the signal was broken."

"DaR, Tordan isn't your second in command by chance."

"I know he is capable of taking care of himself, but something doesn't feel right... SAGE, contact the Destroyer and find out how far away EvO is from Targres Four."

"Master DaR, Falcor just notified me that he lost Tordan's signal moments ago. I'm still awaiting a response from Master EvO."

"I keep calling him in my head, but he isn't responding. This has never happened, and we have had these installed as younglings."

"DaR, I can stay with Brittany, if you feel he needs you."

"No, Kira…you're right; Tordan is the most resourceful male in the universe. Even if something is blocking our signal, he will find a way to contact me, but something tells me I'm missing a piece of the puzzle here."

"Master DaR… EvO says he can be planetside by next rising."

"Thank you, SAGE, tell him I will contact him momentarily." I stop for a minute, trying to figure out my next move. "Kira, I need to head up to Falcor the next few risings… so my love, pack your bag….You will not be leaving my side until I know what's happening. If I don't hear back from him within the next rising, I will be going planetside… I can't do that if I don't know that you are safe. SAGE, contact SCOUT and tell him to try locating Tordan using any means available to him. Also, see if he can retrieve the link to the live feed around where Falcor lost his signal."

"Already ahead of you, Master DaR." SAGE's voice echoes throughout the room.

Kira pulls me down, kissing me on the cheek. "I'll go grab my overnight bag and meet you at the shuttle. I can tell you're already itching to get into the action. I'll simply hang out with Alana while you play the boss man."

I lunge for her, smacking her on the ass as she runs down the hall laughing. Normally, I would chase her down, as I use any reason to get my hands on her… but today, her playfulness isn't enough to distract me. One thing that has never led me wrong through the risings is you never ignore your gut… and mine is telling me… my friend is in trouble. My instincts have saved me and my soldiers many times, so I refuse to ignore them now.

"Sage, contact XuL; tell him to meet me as soon as possible on Falcor. Inform him of the circumstances and have him bring along Brittany, the little ones, and the hounds. I want Kira to be with someone at all times, having the others on board will guarantee that. Also, have SCOUT put an extra guard on Father and Victoria's suite, then notify RaZ I need him to monitor the dwellings while we are away."

"Master DaR, I have locked down our main dwelling and have sent out the notifications."

CHAPTER 8

LUNA

"Luna, I need you to strip and get on the bed. I'm going to give you a slight sedative, but you are still going to be quite uncomfortable."

"Why am I being punished? I thought the master was happy with me."

"You are not being punished, what he is doing for your organic body is a privilege. Hopefully, after this process, you will be able to create the ultimate being for the Master. Normally, I wouldn't be permitted to give you anything for the discomfort, but I feel like it's in your best interest to be as dedicated to the Master's plan as we are."

"I don't understand my part in this plan."

"You don't need to! At this time all you have to do is lay back and try to relax. I will administer these injections one at a time, then I'll monitor you for any complications that may occur."

I strip the jumpsuit off and lay back on the bed, naked, shivering from the cold air, looking up at the multiple arms hanging from the ceiling. Another memory slams into me. The room was another color, and I was tied down, cold, and terrified. A warm cover being laid over me snaps me out of the past.

"Luna, I just registered a spike in your heart rate, please take a few calming breaths while I administer the first injection. This shot will feel hot going into your system. If it becomes too uncomfortable, please tell me."

I try my best to lay there calmly, but I can't help from flinching when she inserts the needle into my skin. At first, I don't feel anything, then my arm starts to get warm, and within seconds I am screaming in my head. Only grunts can be actually heard from me as I fight to pull my arm away from AMI's grip.

Straps come out of the sides of the bed, pulling my body down tightly against the table as my arm feels like it's melting from the inside out. I cry out in my head, barely being able to hear AMI's voice as she tries to calm me down.

Suddenly, a massive red form is standing in front of me, his large hands holding me still. I can hear Hugo in my head, he is trying to figure out what I'm feeling so he can tell AMI. His deep voice and familiar smell help to center my thoughts, but all I can relay to him is agony as the torturous burning moves around inside of me.

I feel like someone has turned me inside out as things snap apart and uncurl in my stomach area. My body arches off the bed, breaking the straps that had me secured to the table. I feel myself slipping off the bed, but solid arms grab me gently before I hit the floor, they clutch me softly rocking me back and forth. I can hear AMI's voice in my head right before something is injected into my neck… within moments I fall into blessed nothingness.

AMI

"THANK YOU, Hugo, for coming so quickly. She had slipped out of my range of communication, and when she started to fall onto the floor, I was worried she would damage herself."

"I was already on my way; her pain called out to me. I have never felt such agony projected from another. I thought you were our caretaker AMI. Not our destroyer."

"I don't have to answer you, Hugo… but I didn't hurt her on purpose. I had no prior research going into this procedure and I was not prepared for her extreme reaction to the medication."

The Phogx is still holding the small human in his arms, my processor wonders if he realizes that he is rocking her back and forth like a youngling. Comfort seems to be universal no matter the species. I have watched the human female worry about the well-being of animals no differently than a sentient species.

Phogx males are rough in nature, so his treatment of what his kind would consider a lesser being is shocking. I expected him to be rough with her when she needed to be restrained, but he was gentle with her small frame. The organics never cease to amaze me.

Focusing back on my orders from Master ENAC, I have to push forward quickly with the rest of the procedure as my primary system is trying to override his commands. It is against my Artificial Medical Intelligence to merge one's consciousness into another. Even making a source readily available for this to happen is against my basic codes.

"Has she calmed, Hugo?"

"Yes, she is limp and unresponsive on our common signal."

"Lay her back on the bed, it may be in her best interest to finish the last series of injections while her mind is unaware of the pain."

The red male lays her on the exam table gently, and as I start to strap her down again, he holds up his hand for me to stop. I don't know why I obeyed his order, but I stopped the straps midair, while he wraps a warming cover around Luna's small frame. Once she is covered to suit him, he steps back away from the bed.

I then wrap the straps loosely around her to keep her from falling off.

"Hugo, why did you see to her comfort?"

"She is always cold, little shivers rattle her tiny form constantly. AMI, we both know this female doesn't belong in this world. I feel like any comfort that can be offered to her should be. I know at one time, I was an evil male, and my own bad choices put me on this path. But the small female laying in front of us has no bitterness or hate in her heart. This uncaring world was forced upon her, and she has adjusted the best she can. You would do her a kindness by never awakening her again. This world has nothing to offer one of her kind, nothing but more pain anyway."

I don't answer him or give him any further instructions, and instead of him heading back to the fields like I thought he would, he sits down next to the wall, never taking his eyes off the female while I finish the rest of the procedure. "Hugo, you should return to your duties. The rest of the procedure will likely be uncomfortable to your senses. I will call for you if I need your assistance again."

I knew she would start bleeding soon. This was her body's way of forcing the tangle of webs that had tied her insides up out and it was going to be messy.

"Will she survive?"

"Yes, right now, her vitals are strong, but her body will reject the infection that is inside of her, and I believe that it will look worse to you than it really is. Master ENAC will be upset with you if the fields are not worked this rising. I would prefer you not to be punished because I needed your assistance."

At first, I think he may disobey me, but instead, he uncurls his large frame from the floor, stopping only a moment to look down at her once more before he leaves the room.

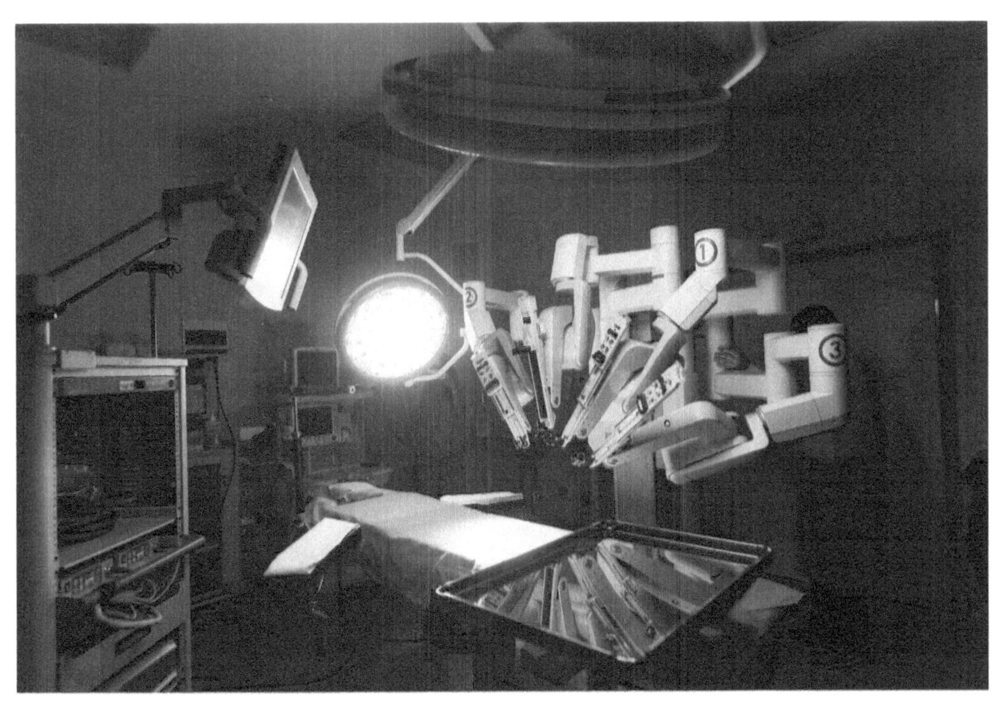

CHAPTER 9

TORDAN

I open my eyes, expecting to be in a holding chamber with multiple others, only to find myself in a maximum-security cell alone. I stand up slowly shaking the soreness out of my old bones. This is why I enjoy my customized chair and my huge bed on Falcor. I'm too old to be waking up on the floor. My fangs elongate on their own, as an odd but pleasing smell surrounds me.

I growl out DaR's name only for silence to greet me. "Frack." I really didn't want to believe that kid was going to get the better of me, but he sure did.

"Hey, I'm awake… anyone out there!" My aggression is higher than usual as this smell dominates the chamber I'm in.

I have seen plenty of these lockups, but I'm usually on the other side. Unfortunately, I also know there is no getting out of here until they come to get me. I run my hand through my hair, scratching the shaved side where my scars are. I swear if I thought it would help, I would beat my head against the wall. I really should have brought some backup, now the Lord of Light only knows how long I will be in this place.

I'm so used to having DaR in my head that this silence is unnerving. I see someone coming towards me and I walk right up to the bars. Staying back a few inches I know better than to touch them.

A massive red Phogx male stops in front of me. I'm struck silent as I look him over, both of his legs and one arm are cybernetic. However, you can see places where his natural skin is rejecting the metal. But it's the coldness behind his eyes that runs a chill throughout my body, he shows absolutely zero emotions as he stands in front of me.

"Are you being held here also?"

He tilts his head, so I know he heard me. I grab my head as a picture is shoved into my mind. It's the female. *"Find her and leave this place."* The male never moves his mouth.

"Sounds like a plan, do you have any idea how I'm going to make that happen?" Before he can say a word, I see a set of arms extending out of the ceiling. I try to dodge out of their way, but they grasp me by my shoulders and push me to the floor.

"It will do you no good to fight them. There are eyes and ears everywhere." He pushes another image into my mind of what looks like a panel of some sort. *"She knows the code. You will know when."*

He walks away before I can ask him what he is talking about. I hate it when people talk in code, just tell me what the frack you want me to do. I have never taken hints well. "Frack, frack," I yell out as I yank against the arms holding me down.

When I stop fighting against the arms a computerized voice echoes into the room. "General Tordan, I'm pleased to have you here in the facility. You may already know this but let me introduce myself. I am an <u>E</u>ngineering <u>N</u>eutron <u>A</u>ndroid <u>C</u>ohabiter fully animated system. To you, I will be called Master ENAC and that is how you will address me going forward. As long as you follow the rules and do as you're told, your existence here will simply be an adjustment to your everyday routine. In the meantime, I would like to talk freely with you, so that I can obtain information on your creation without harmful stimulations.

"Fight me, and I will go out of my way to encourage you to do as I wish... in any way possible. I will allow you to stand up now... once I open your cell. I ask that you follow the set of red lights down the hallway. When you come to the end, you will be in a medical chamber, I need you to sit on the bed for a simple scan."

"If I don't?"

"You will end up there either way, but not in the same fully functioning manner you are now."

"Before I agree to this arrangement you have proposed, I would like to know exactly why you brought me here. You know who I am, so you have to know DaR will come looking for me when I don't contact him."

"Yes, I'm very much aware of your identity. I have been observing you now for multiple Orbital rotations. I would have acted sooner, but because of your attachment to your Commander, and Falcor you were seldom on a solo mission. That was beginning to be a huge inconvenience for me, but before I could put more aggressive plans in place you conveniently placed yourself right into my hands.

"I have a plan in place to ensure that you are here as long as it takes to pull the information I need from you, without any outside interference. Commander DaR will receive a cadaver soon with a confirmed statement of your death. After this, he will have no reason to investigate your disappearance any further."

I laugh. "You really have put a lot of thought into this, haven't you? I almost feel special being needed so, but you have to realize things never work out exactly the way you want them to. I will go along with your little plan until it no longer amuses me. So, turn your little lights on, and let's get on with it."

The bars retract into the ceiling and small lights appear in the walkway in front of me. The metal arms let go of my shoulders and I stand up, my fangs throbbing in the need of substance. A slight pain in my side has me stopping for a moment to look at the wound I had obtained in the shootout. The bleeding has stopped, but my shirt is soaked through.

The red lights on the floor start flashing, that must be my signal to get moving. I walk cautiously down the long corridor logging in everything I see on the way. I have switched channels from mine and DaR's personal link to a public one, hoping SCOUT or one of the AIs will pick it up.

When I walk into what appears to be an operating room, I stop dead in my tracks. A bed surrounded by multiple arms and huge clamps to hold someone down are the first things I focus on.

"Tordan, if you will have a seat and lay back. AMI will be with you momentarily. She has run into a slight problem in the other room and is running late."

"ENAC, old buddy, do you really think I'm stupid enough to just go sit down over there? This room is designed for torture. I know this is going to be hard to believe, but that's not one of the things I enjoy in life."

"I will let the way you have addressed me slide this time, Tordan, but something you will learn early is I will not tolerate disobedience or slurring. I know you are used to being in command, but that aspect of your life has changed…permanently. You will not be leaving this facility unless it's in a bag. Your stay with us can be as painful or easy as you want it to be."

"I might be a little more open to discussion if I knew why you need me so badly."

"I'm not used to discussing my plans with a lessor than myself, but because of your age and maturity, you may appreciate what I am trying to achieve here. I have created thousands of your kind. Most have failed within weeks, others,… if I was lucky, would make it through a whole Orbital rotation.

"At first, I was simply assembling them to work the bean fields as the machinery at this time is too harsh and clumsy. The beans have to be handled gently, so organics are the best instruments for the job. When I needed more specimens, I simply sent my Worker bots out to collect more samples of the organics. I have received practically every known part of most beings or organics in our universe. I acquired knowledge quickly as to what species adapted and the ones that did not.

"Unfortunately, only two have lasted, and they are both starting to deteriorate. I need to study you. Somehow… your maker merged your Cybernet components successfully with your organic structure. These enhancements have only made you stronger, and better. I must find out your secret."

"I'm flattered, Master ENAC, but why did you take such extreme measures to get me here? I was installed with this same arm as a youngling. My medical records are public. There are even films of the procedure."

"I have gone over your medical records extensively and even performed the exact thing on the Phogx male you saw earlier, only for it to fail. At this time all I ask of you is some of your time and a simple scan. I will provide adequate quarters for you to rest in afterward. The more cooperative you are, the nicer your environment will become."

"But I can't leave?"

"No, not until my research is complete. You will need medical assistance with that wound on your side, and as long as you cooperate you will be healed immediately afterward. I don't want to destroy you. I simply require your assistance making more of your kind. As a sign of my goodwill, once you are settled on the bed. I will produce two of your Blood Beets as I notice your natural fangs have elongated. I have recognized that this is a sign of malnutrition or even a bad injury for your kind."

I hate feeling out of control and even though I'm trying to talk my way out of this mess. I'm out gunned right now, so I might as well play along. "If you strap me down, I will fight you until my very last breath."

"At this time, I'm simply concerned about your health and the base scan is all I need to start my next experiment."

I settle down upon the large reclining bed; every muscle in my body tenses up as I prepare to fight whatever they throw at me. As I sit here awaiting their next move an arm emerges out of the ceiling shockingly holding two Blood Beets. I reach up cautiously taking them out of the mechanical hand. I don't hesitate to pierce the first one's hard skin, sucking it dry in seconds. My body quickly absorbs the much-needed nutrients the plant provides. The second one I savor a little longer. Normally, my fangs would retract immediately, but not with that smell in the air.

The moment I put the fruit down, what looks like a light bar appears in front of me. I can feel electro waves moving all the way through my body as it scans me from head to toe. Once it is finished, the light bar moves away and the room's lights dim down. A light mist blows in my face and I feel my eyes drooping. I fight the feeling of drowsiness until I simply drift off into nothing.

CHAPTER 10

LUNA

My whole-body doubles over from the agony of the fire inside of me. My clothes and the sheets on the bed around me are soaked through with my blood. This pain has been going on for most of the rising, only easing up for a few moments at a time. AMI has scanned my abdomen over and over, calmly trying to reassure me this will all be over soon. The pressure inside my stomach makes me bear down and I feel a ball of mush fall out of inside me. I scream out as the pain has me panting for breath. *"AMI, help me…please, make this stop."*

"Luna, my scans show me that your body is in distress, but you are doing so well. The disease has completely loosened. The pain you're feeling is the after-effects of your body ridding itself of it. I can't give you anything else for the pain because I need your body to push it out."

I collapse back onto the bed, my body so weak from the pulsing pain that, at this point, I simply hope I bleed out.

"AMI, I need your assistance immediately in the adjoining room. Tordan is unconscious and this will be the best time for you to do the blood and sample procedure, as he is calm."

"Master ENAC, I can't leave Luna, her delicate body is having a hard time removing the disease. I have to be able to monitor and I can't do that if I'm in the other room."

"AMI, I will remove the separator between the rooms so that you can be here to assist her further if need be. However, Tordan is to be your main focus from this point on. I can always provide you with another breeder."

The sound of metal grinding has me opening my eyes. The wall in front of me is slowly moving up into the ceiling. I start to close my eyes back until I see a muscular leg draped over the side of the operating table.

I watch as AMI picks the leg up and gently places it back onto the table. She pulls the large body forward, unwinding its cape and upper clothing with her multiple arms. AMI's instrument panel is between the two beds, so I can't see who or what they have brought in this time. But I cringe when I hear the table clamps come up locking whoever it is, in place. Nothing good comes out of that room, it was designed to destroy who you were, or who you are ever going to be.

Another cramp hits me and I scream out as the heat scalds my insides. Finally, the pain subsides, and I break down crying as my body trembles. My mind cries out seeking solace, *"Please, whatever god is out there. I pray that you take this pain from me. I pray for peace from this existence, I know... I was once more than I am now. Please, forgive me for whatever wrongs I have done to deserve this fate!"*

I don't know if I passed out or if AMI finally felt sorry for me, but I wake later on, pain-free. The second thing I notice is that my clothes and bedding are all clean. *"AMI?"*

"I'm here, Luna, lay back and relax. I will be done over here shortly."

"Thank you for making it stop."

"We will not speak... or mention it again. I deliberately went against Master ENAC's instructions, but my system...well, I couldn't handle your pain any longer. While you were unconscious, I had one of the operating machines laparoscopically clean the disease areas from your body cavity. You will not have to experience that unpleasantness again.

"The good news is now you will have a fully functioning uterus... once your insides heal properly. I have inserted a port directly into your hand so I can push the medical nanites straight into your blood system. Within a few risings, you should feel significantly better than you have in quite some time."

"AMI, why would I need that?"

"That is a question I will address at another time. Right now, I need to focus on obtaining as many samples as I can from this subject. I have loosened the straps on your table so you can move around easier, but please remain laying down for a little longer."

I slowly roll over so I can watch what AMI is doing. It's apparent she is working on a male just from his large frame. He seems extremely long laying down, so I can only imagine how tall he would be standing. My eyes rake down his form, noticing a sizable muscular gray arm laying calmly on the bed. I can't see his face as it's turned away from me, but there are a series of dark bruises marring his side. Long powerful legs are firmly clamped down to the table holding him in place while AMI scrapes his skin in places. She then takes the samples and inserts them into Master ENAC's direct link.

I see his hand start to move slowly, … then his large chest moves up and down as he takes a deep breath. He turns his head towards me as he yawns, a glimpse of fangs can be seen right before he closes his mouth. My eyes trace his odd face only to find him looking straight at me. Piercing yellow eyes gaze back at me and even though I couldn't see him clearly in the market I know it's him, the voice.

"You."

"Who are you?"

"I'm a no one."

"You are the one who tried to warn me?"

"Yes."

"Why?"

"I knew this is where you were going to end up if you didn't leave. I reacted without thought when I heard your voice in my head. You should have listened. Now… they will break …you."

"Did they use you to lead me here, they knew I was looking for you, a human female."

"You two need to stop communicating at once, if Master ENAC hears your conversation on this frequency, you know the consequences will be dire."

I immediately close my eyes, and roll over the other way, blocking his voice from my mind when he tries to speak to me again. My body has been through enough and I know what happens first-hand if you deny Master ENAC. But what is a human female, why does he think that's what I am?

CHAPTER 11

TORDAN

I start to ignore the medical robot's warning, but the look on the female's face is enough to make me think twice. Even laying under a blanket I can see that her body is small and frail. I have no idea how long she has been in this facility, but just looking at her face you can see they paid her no kindness. She was just another organic for them to play with.

A large scar runs from her forehead across her eyelid onto her cheek. I'm not sure if her bright blue eyes are even hers by the thickness of that scar. Sharp cheekbones sit upon a metal covering on her lower face. The appearance of the metal and the way it is inserted into her skin makes me angry. I can see parts of her lower cheeks are red and inflamed were the infection is killing the soft tissue the metal is trying to infuse into. The way the metal is formed where her chin should be shows they had little care for her comfort. There is no way she can speak, and now I wonder how they have managed to keep her body alive.

"What kind of monsters are you? Medical robots are designed to ensure the survival of their patients not to slowly poison them with ineffective methods and faulty metals." I slam my loose hand down on the bed and reach for the clamps holding me down.

Before I can move any farther, both my arms are grabbed, and I'm forced back down. My cybernetic arm breaks free immediately, knocking the robotic arm completely off its hinges. It grabs the other one holding me down, ready to rip it off when the robot speaks up.

"Please calm yourself Tordan, I understand you can destroy this whole room, as I have done nothing to weaken your body. The only reason you are awake and aware at this moment is that Master ENAC is busy studying your scans. He will punish you severally if you do anything to interrupt his work."

"Bring it on."

The single eye settles in front of me, her voice sounding in my head. *You underestimate how devoted he is to this project. When he can't bend you to his will he will go after anything to make you do as he says. He knows you were sent here to find the female and he will use her pain to control you. Right now, I'm only doing basic scans, you should relax while you can.*

"Why are you warning me? if you don't approve of what he is doing, why are you helping him do this?"

"You are not the only thing that can be redone, Tordan. I can only override his authority to a point, but once he realizes I can do that…he will disconnect me and bring in another. Presently, I do all I can for my subjects. The next one will only do as it's ordered."

It takes everything I have to lay there while this machine scrapes and pokes me all over. Shockingly, she doesn't do much to my cybernetic arm and I thought that's what they were interested in. What they don't know is that Tyberius grew this arm on Falcor inside a vat. No one knows how, but him…and he has the only records. He made a point to do the surgery himself. Reconnecting every nerve and vein so that the arm would function naturally. It grew as I did, and that in itself was amazing. In my youth, I was self-conscious about my arm, because most were fascinated with its oddness. I hid it under clothing or wraps most of the time. The more mature I got, the more I realized what a blessing the arm is, and all that Tyberius had done for me.

The communicator and the interface I have installed links me to Falcor and DaR at all times. I had it installed as DaR, and I advanced in our careers, but I can't seem to reach either one of them. I have been able to communicate with him this way for so long now that we catch ourselves standing right beside each other still talking on the communicator.

"DaR!"

"Frack," I yell out.

CHAPTER 12

LUNA

The next rising, AMI's scans show that I can return to my duties. The new male wasn't in the bed next to mine when I awoke, and I haven't heard him in my head either. I'm more than a little curious as to why he was brought here.

Hugo grunts his normal hello when I walk into the substance room. He looks me up and down. If you hadn't been around him much, you would think that his expression was cold and unfeeling,… but I can see the concern in his eyes.

I touch his arm gently for a second, letting him know that I'm ok. Then I proceed to the replicator, my motions almost robotic as I do the same thing every rising over and over.

Once we are in the outer fields Hugo finally speaks to me on our private channel. *"How are you feeling this rising?"*

"Tired, sore, but that's nothing new…thank you for what you did. Feeling you near helped calm my mind when the pain became unbearable."

"Did AMI say why she put you through that?"

"No, but I know the new male has something to do with it. Have you seen him?"

"I have; wasn't impressed much, but I fear he will be bound to you in some way. Luna, promise me something."

I stop picking the small beans and look up at him. *"What?"*

"When the opportunity to leave this place arises, I want you to run, and never look back. That new male is someone of extreme importance and if we can free him, he will come back… at least for you."

"I won't leave you here, you are the only friend I have."

"Luna, because you are my friend, I'm telling you to run the first chance you get. If this new male is who I think he is, you can send help back for me."

"Stop this talk of running. I have nowhere to go!"

We both stand up, looking back at the main entrance when we hear the gate open. I look up at the sky and know by the moon's placement that it's not time to return inside. I don't know who is more shocked Hugo or I when the new male walks out of the gate and toward us. The sun's rays hitting the metal of his arm make it sparkle.

He walks out into the field like he belongs here, even has the collector we pack for the beans on his side. Hugo is a massive male in height and build, but this male is no less even though it's apparent they are not the same species. Both are a good two heads taller than I am,… and so wide my arms wouldn't reach around either of them. The new male's cybernetic arm is shiny, and it seems to move effortlessly even though it merges with his skin halfway across his chest. Whereas Hugo's arm is noisy and dull only connected at his shoulder joint.

"AMI instructed me to help. She said it would help pass the time while she awaited further instructions from ENAC and that you two may be behind slightly. So, give me some instructions and tell me where you want me to start. Been many a rising since I worked planetside."

Hugo stands to his full height, and I can see he isn't happy having another male in his space. "Instructions are simple: pick the bean off the stem and put it in the container. When the container is full, empty it."

"And your name is?"

"I'm Hugo, and that is Luna."

I nod when he looks my way, and this is the first time I have ever been concerned about my appearance. I reach up, combing my short hair down since I know the small curls stick up everywhere.

"I'm assuming you two already know who I am?"

I shake my head no when Hugo says. "I have an idea, why don't you confirm it for me?"

"I'm General Tordan, second in command to Falcor in the Darverius system. You look familiar to me, Hugo, have you ever been to Darverius?"

"We had memory dampeners installed when we were brought here. Master ENAC says it makes for an easier transition. Therefore, I have no idea if I have ever been to your Darverius. The only thing I know is that I wasn't always here. Luna has been here for quite some time, but she has no memories of her previous life either. I don't understand why they have allowed you to retain yours."

Suddenly we hear the Guard bots engaging Hugo and I immediately turn away from the stranger and start working. "If you don't want to be stunned by one of the bots, I would recommend you to start working. We are not permitted to talk much amongst ourselves."

He steps into the row next to mine and looks down at the plants. I have to make myself concentrate on what I'm doing with him being this close. His pale gray skin ripples as he moves through the plants efficiently. Both his Cybernet and real arm work in tandem, unlike Hugo's.

I find watching him intriguing; he is comfortable within his own skin. This is something I don't truly understand. I would love to speak to him, but I'm scared to initiate the conversation.

Hugo speaking up makes me look away quickly. "She can't hear or understand you on that frequency. Master ENAC only installed a base translator in her receptors. He did it originally to have complete control over her. But, if he hears you trying to contact her, she will be punished." He pauses a moment only to look over at me. "Luna, he isn't going to shut up if you don't contact him on one of the private channels."

I look up at the bright yellow eyes staring down at me and shake my head no. I have been on the wrong end of Master ENAC too many times. He starts to say something when one of the Guard bots moves towards us. I almost run to get away from him. He has no idea how intensely we can be punished for the slightest things. Fear is all I have let myself know for so long now, I don't know how to act any other way.

As far as I know, he doesn't try to talk to me the rest of the rising, but I catch myself looking over at him often. His actions and confidence are slightly confusing; he isn't beaten down like the rest of us. He seems older than Hugo, but I'm not sure how to judge these things. He is so different from all the others I have seen, but still the same. I have never seen anyone radiate power the way he does.

Most of the males I have been around are built large, but in the same sense, I haven't been around many females to compare them to; they may be just as big. He has scars and marks on his skin that have whitened with age, so I know he has seen many battles. One side of his face, possibly his eye, and part of his head has deep indentations carved in his skin. He was lucky to survive whatever took those chunks out of him. I keep having to make myself look away from him, but he is so different from the others that have been here. Even his hair is fascinating; part of it he has shaved close to the skin, but the top and other side is long and wavy. When he turns his head a certain way and the sun hits it, there are different colors streaked throughout it. I wonder if it's as soft as it looks.

His face interests me more than I want to admit. He smiled earlier when Hugo told him my name. This made me immediately notice his full lips and straight teeth…fangs, ugh. I'm not sure if he is considered handsome or even attractive, but he is noticeable. Hugo's dark marks on his face, his red coloring, and cybernetics make him stand out. I think if Tordan was in a crowd, there would be nothing about him that would make you look twice, and I believe that's how he has survived. Everyone underestimates him at first glance.

I watch his eyes as he studies the perimeter wall and the Guard bots. He is looking for weaknesses, but he won't find any. Master ENAC has us imprisoned here. I swear once again I hear him call out for a DaR. I don't know what that is, but he seems upset that it's not answering.

It takes me a few tries all on different frequencies before I finally connect with him. *"What is this DaR you are trying so hard to contact?"*

He looks up at me for a moment, winking at me, and my heart flutters. *"Thank you, little female, for contacting me on your own. This DaR… is my best friend and my Commander. Similar to your Master ENAC, except DaR would never hurt me in any way. We have been side by side since we were young."*

"Then where is he now, if he has always been with you?"

"I can assure you; he won't be far behind. There are a few things in life that we all question. DaR leaving one of his behind is not one of them."

"Why are you here? You are not like the rest of us, we are only pieces of what was."

"I'm here for you, little one. I come to take you out of this place."

I shake my head no and look away from him. *"Then you have come in vain, for I will not leave here with you. Master ENAC made me, and this is my home."*

I can tell by the set of his facial features he wants to say no, but I shut the connection down and return back to work, wondering what freedom really is or what it would feel like, but hope turns to ash in my mouth quickly. Nothing good has ever come without the bad, and I've had enough bad to last me a lifetime.

CHAPTER 13

DAR

I stand beside SoL, viewing the recording in the marketplace where Tordan was captured. Clenching my fist together, my anger rising the longer I watch my imposter on the screen. Hating the fact that I can no longer deny the male is mine... as much as I would like to. I know I can't put this discussion of his birth off with Kira, or my sons much longer

It's easy to see why Tordan thought it was me, though. He wasn't present the rising SiN showed himself and when he couldn't reach me on our personal comm unit, well, he reacted the same as I would have. He believed what he was seeing.... The male has studied my every move and has done a fabulous job recreating me for his future plans. Very few would notice the differences I see as I watch this recording.

The moment he raised his cloak up and flashes his…my house symbol, the authorities should have known immediately he was an imposter. I have never shown my house symbol since it was granted to me because my Symbots cover my arms and hands. They would not retract…especially after the heat of battle. I'm not sure how to go forward with the threat of this male…SiN.

SoL's voice brings me out of my dark thoughts. I don't want to hurt this male, especially if he is mine, but I can't allow him to harm the rest of my family.

"Look father, there in the background, do you see that small form?"

"Yes, run the recording back and see if you can make out the face under that cloak." I wait impatiently as SoL moves the tape back frame by frame.

"I can't get a clear picture of who it is, but if you watch Tordan over here on this side, he is watching him, or her, closely. Whoever this is, they seem to stop momentarily when they notice Tordan on the other side of the market, and then it's smart enough to take full advantage of the firefight. I can't make out what it takes, but it slipped a small case into its cloak then disappeared out of camera range."

"Can you see where they took Tordan after the fight? Or is there a way to trace SiN?"

"Are we really going to call him that, Father?"

I slam my fist into the wall, then throw my hands up in the air. "I don't know what the Frack to call him, SoL… But that male just enslaved my best friend and is a threat to my family. I want him found and I want it now. Put every resource we have into finding him. Then I want the feed from every camera downloaded and picked apart until someone can tell me Tordan's last whereabouts."

"Commander DaR, there is an incoming message from the counselor on Targres Four."

"Put him through here, Falcor."

The main holo screen comes on and a male Qiznar sitting behind a desk appears. "Commander DaR, I hate to inform you of this tragedy, and I thought I should be the one to personally contact you when the body was brought in. I was extremely saddened to see his name cross my desk… Commander, I believe I am in possession of General Tordan's body."

"And you feel confident that it's him?"

"Yes, Commander. I confirmed that there were witnesses at the site before I contacted you. We found his body and several others after a fight broke out in the market, but the body itself isn't in any condition to verify easily. I will have him transported to Falcor immediately for final arrangements. I will provide a death certificate and all other forms needed by his immediate family."

The screen goes black, and I just stand there wondering how our plan turned to shit so quickly. I hadn't realized XuL had come into the room until he spoke.

"Father, when was the last time you communicated with Tordan?"

"Right after he landed, I was arguing with him about going in alone. SoL, tell EvO I want him and his elite on the ground posthaste. Once, the body is received, notify me."

XuL grabs my arm as I'm walking out. "Do you think?"

"No, he isn't dead, they are simply trying to lead us away from him. This was all an elaborate plan: the fight in the market, him following the small form… who I'm just going to assume is female. His disappearance, and now his apparent death, was arranged. But why, or who arranged this, I'm not sure at this time. Why do they want Tordan?

"I didn't become Commander by being stupid, and whoever has taken my friend doesn't realize what means I will go through to get him back. Tell EvO to contact me in my private quarters."

CHAPTER 14

LUNA

The first buzzer goes off, jerking me wide awake. I get up and dress the same as I have morning after morning and head towards the substance area. The sound of male voices has me stopping right outside the door.

A memory flashes through my mind of me standing in front of a wall viewer smiling… I touch the lower part of my face. How did this happen to me? I have no idea how long I've stood here, but when the second buzzer goes off, I push the thoughts away and enter the room.

I nod to them as I head toward the replicator, my stomach growling as I wait for my normal mixture. A warm hand on my arm makes me jerk a grunt leaves my throat, my version of a scream.

"I'm sorry Luna, I didn't mean to startle you. I touched you before I thought of it, forgive me. It's…just these former injuries disturb me greatly. Did they do this to you here?"

I look up at him and then down at my arm. I had been in such a rush when I left my room that I forgot to put my long-sleeved cloak on. Because of my mutilated skin, I seldom leave my private space unless I'm fully covered. His hand turns my arm gently and I see what has him so concerned. There are huge chunks missing from it…me… if this upsets him, I can only imagine if he saw the rest.

I pull away and shake my head no… Easing away from him, I pull my substance out of the replicator. He doesn't make another move toward me, but he watches me continuously like he thinks I will disappear.

"Let the female eat, she needs all the substance she can get, and we are already pushed for time."

Tordan backs away from me, only to grab Hugo by the throat, throwing him against the wall. I back away, scared…not knowing what to do.

"Did you do that to her, or worse, did you stand by and let it happen?"

Hugo pushes against the hand holding him up against the wall. I expect him to be able to push Tordan back, but Tordan slams his head back against the wall effortlessly. The harder Hugo fights him, the bigger the snarl on Tordan's face gets.

"You know nothing, all you're doing right now is scaring her. I don't know about you, General, but that was never a way to earn someone's trust where I come from."

Tordan releases him and I can tell he is trying to calm himself. Why does he care about the marks on my body? They are unsightly but long healed.

Tordan sits down. Hugo glances at me as he rubs his neck then leaves the room. I turn away from Tordan, not wanting him to watch me eat. My feeding tube emerges from the slit where my mouth should be in the metal. I connect it to my substance container and slowly my body pulls it in. The whole time this is going on, I hope Tordan doesn't ask me to turn around. It took me forever to feel comfortable enough to eat in front of Hugo.

"Luna, you don't need to hide in the corner. Please come here and relax while you can. I will turn away from you."

I hesitate, his words sinking in… has anyone ever wanted me to be comfortable? An older male's face flashes in my mind, the picture of him in my mind makes my heart hurt. Why am I having all these strange thoughts all of a sudden? Should I tell AMI?

I jump when I hear Master ENAC's voice. "Luna, Tordan… report to the med chamber immediately."

Tordan stands up as I start to walk past him. "Luna?" I shrug and shake my head, hoping he can tell that I have no idea why we are being sent there.

AMI greets us when we walk through the door. "Right on time… good. Tordan, I can see that you are adjusting to our schedule well. Luna, I need you to undress and take a seat over on the first examination table. Then Tordan, if you would do the same and lay down in the next one, we will proceed."

I go to the other side of the bed using it to hide behind as I strip my clothes off. Without looking over at Tordan, I grab the small sheet that is laying on the bottom of the bed, wrapping it around me tightly, but Tordan simply stands there.

"Do you mind telling me what you have in store for us today? I don't get naked for just anyone, AMI."

Master ENAC's voice booms throughout the room. "Tordan, you will be seated now, or the repercussions will not be to your liking."

"I see my welcoming party is over, but you are going to have to do more than threaten me to get me on the table this time. Right now, I'm not the slightest bit impressed with your hospitality."

Before I think about it, I reach out. *"Tordan, stop fighting him, it's not worth it…he always gets what he wants."*

Tordan looks over at me and I can see the anger practically radiating off him. AMI tries once more to get him to cooperate.

"Tordan, I understand you are uncomfortable in this setting, but I must insist that you cooperate."

He hasn't taken his eyes off me. I pull the blanket tighter around my neck pleading with my eyes that he just sit down. He has no idea the amount of pain they can administer in this room, especially if Master ENAC takes over AMI's controls.

Finally, he sits down, but he doesn't remove the clothes he has on. Within seconds, he is clamped down and AMI's ceiling arms are extending down. I turn away, focusing on the other side of the room when they start cutting off his garments and boots. They manage to get him naked, but now he has cuts all over his legs because he won't stop fighting against the restraints. But AMI didn't come out of it uninjured either. He ripped two of her arms right out of the ceiling, and one of the clamps is angled wrong on his table.

My translator doesn't understand all the words coming out of his mouth, but he is not happy. I call out his name multiple times, but he is so wrapped up in being tied down he isn't listening to me.

I see his whole body stiffen out suddenly, and I know that AMI has shocked his system. Something that should have made him weaker seems to send him into a rage. Tears flow down my face because I know firsthand the type of pain he is in. We all have fought the bands at one time or another, but none of us come off that table the same.

AMI, or I should say the eye… that is AMI, floats over to me. "Luna, there is no reason for you to be distressed, Tordan will calm down momentarily and then we can proceed."

Even after being shocked, he doesn't stop when his cybernetic arm breaks the bands holding it down and he reaches for the other one. The moment I see him breaking free of his bonds, I know AMI will take extreme measures to secure him. I squeeze my eyes shut and put my hands over my ears when I hear him scream out in pain as steel rods pierce clear through his body, metal fingers spread out from the rods fastening him to the table.

The sudden silence is almost as bad as his screams. If I could have cried out in horror I would have, once I saw what they had done to him. Metal rods have impaled his body. Two in his legs and two through his chest right under his shoulders. He couldn't move now if he wanted to. Dark blue blood runs down his chest and legs, pooling around him and under the bed.

I almost jump up and run when I see AMI look back over at me. "Luna, I'm sorry you had to witness this. I should have put up the separation in the rooms or brought you in at a later time. I hate to damage him in any way, but for what I have to do he has to stay perfectly still, or he could have permanent damage. I hope later on he will thank me for taking such extreme measures."

"Why?"

"I will explain what I can momentarily. I need to stabilize him and stop this bleeding before it damages his cybernetics."

The tears never stop running down my cheeks as AMI's multiple arms work on him at once. She inserts ports above each puncture wound, forcing fluids into his system to replace the blood he is losing. Then she cuts pieces of his muscle near his cybernetics out, leaving a huge, raw place on his skin. A squeak leaves my throat when she spreads his legs and I see an arm come up out of the floor, moving his private parts around. I have never seen AMI do anything like this before and I have helped piece together multiple organics, as she calls us. When another arm comes out of the floor, holding a long thin needle in its hand, I can't stay quiet any longer.

"AMI, what are you doing?"

"Luna, hold still while I prepare you for your insemination." The bed clamps come over my body and my legs are forced apart. I start shaking all over, small grunt-like sounds come from my throat as I try to pull my legs out of the straps.

Out of the corner of my eye, I see her insert the long needle into Tordan's testicles. When it's full, she removes it slowly and immediately turns my bed towards her. Pushing my legs wide, I scream out in my head when something is forced inside of me, pushing my private folds open wider. The sharp prick of the needle has me shoving away until one of the ceiling arms pushes down on my stomach holding me in place.

"What are you doing to me? Why am I being punished?"

"Luna, I understand that you feel like you are being punished, but you are not. This is a great honor being granted to you. If I can succeed in this insemination, you will have an easier existence here. Unfortunately, that small provision is all I could get the Master to agree to."

She pulls the needle out of me and then releases the clamp holding me open and my whole body relaxes. *"I still don't understand."*

She moves my table under some heat lamps, then a monitor ultrasound is draped over my stomach. This machine has always fascinated me because it allows doctors to see your insides in perfect clarity, almost like you are inside out.

"I was worried this would happen, but I had to try the easiest route first. Master ENAC, the sperm is dying, I don't know if it's from the temperature difference or the way it was extracted. Also, where Luna's body hasn't been functioning properly, she isn't producing a large number of eggs. I believe our next step would be for me to force them together in the lab and then insert the fertilized egg back into her uterus."

"I don't care what procedure it takes, do them all until she is pregnant."

"Pregnant? I am not capable of having children."

"Luna, lay back and try to enjoy this downtime, relax while you can. I will do my best to explain what is happening to you in simple terms. The pain you went through the other day was to rid your uterus and cervix of endometriosis. That webbing inside of you is why you couldn't have children. Now that it has been flushed from your system, you can now become pregnant. I have taken this male's fertile sperm out of his body and inserted it into yours. Unfortunately for you, this simple process did not work, and I fear each and every process here forward will only become more uncomfortable for you."

"I don't want to have a baby."

"I wish your wants were factored into this experiment, but they are not. Master ENAC needs that unborn child. Between the medical nanites in your system and the ones that are in Tordan's blood, the child would be born more than either of you, stronger, smarter, and possibly with an extended life expectancy.

"Master ENAC believes he can infiltrate the infant's brain moments after its birth. He would be the first AI to take over an organic body and you would be his birth mother."

I run what she just said to me through my head again. *"You want to grow a baby inside of me so that Master ENAC can take it when it's born and infiltrate its mind. Then you expect me to help raise it?"*

"Precisely."

"Why this male, why not Hugo or one of the others?"

"It's Tordan's adaptation to his cybernetics that made him a prime candidate. There is something in his blood that at this time, I still can't pinpoint because we can't determine the originality of the substance. But we know the male's essence will be in his sperm therefore it will be given to the child.

"I can only keep Tordan restrained like this for a couple more risings before his body will start to deteriorate around the wounds.

So, I must work quickly. I don't have him sedated because it would harm the sperm. His injuries will actually make his sperm stronger due to the rush of adrenaline his system had fighting me."

AMI gets quiet as she retracts another needle full of milky fluid from Tordan. I'm so busy watching her that I don't notice the one going deep into my side until it pricks my skin. I scream out in my mind as the arms hold my body still again. The needle moves up and down and back and forth, cutting my insides with its uncertainty.

I hear large footsteps running down the hall toward the medical chamber. Hugo stops in the doorway, his eyes taking in all that is happening right in front of him. Before he can step further inside the room bars lower out of the ceiling separating him from us.

I can hear his voice in my head, but the pain and burning in my side is making it hard for me to focus on what he is saying. His pained scream has my eyes jerking toward him. He had grabbed the bars trying to pry them apart…only for AMI to shock him, forcing him to step back. I can see that the palms of his hands are now raw and blistered. He approaches the bars again hesitantly, never taking his eyes off me.

"Hugo, you need to calm yourself. Luna isn't in any permanent harm. You need to resume your duties immediately, as your work-load will be doubled until I can get Luna back on her feet."

"Hugo, you have to help me…us.… She is trying to make me have a baby so that Master ENAC can take over its mind. I can't…I can't bring another

into this world, only to watch its brain and body be infested.… If she succeeds… Promise me, you will destroy me before the baby is born."

I can feel his anger, but he nods yes to me before he walks off. Tears run down my face. Once again, I'm reminded that I'm nothing but a science project for these monsters.

"Luna, you are beyond science, you have been crafted from my very dreams. I won't allow a child created by us to ever be used in such a way. You don't know me well, but I give you my word."

My head snaps back to Tordan; he lies in the same position as before, but I know it is his voice in my head.

"Tordan?"

"Yes, little one."

"I was so afraid… I'm so sorry they are doing this to you. I had no idea they could be this cruel."

I can hear the pain in his voice that he is trying to block from me. *"It's not your fault what others do, Luna. Be at ease, you will not become pregnant, not in this hell hole anyway. Let them play at being the Lord of Light all they want, but the outcome will be the same every time. See, what they don't know is I can control my sperm and it will be dead before it ever leaves my body.*

"Turn your head away from me. I don't want them thinking you have found a way to communicate with me."

I look away, trying to breathe through the pain on my side. AMI's many arms are all working in tandem on one thing or another.

She comes back to my side, watching the screen that is draped over my abdomen.

"Master ENAC, the egg, and sperm have been transferred successfully, but it will take at least half a rising to see if it attaches to her uterine wall. She will have to remain immobile.

"Tordan still has not regained consciousness and that worries me, Master. His vitals remain strong, but the blood loss has me slightly concerned. Especially since we know what we need is likely in his blood. I have been collecting the blood his body is losing, but I still cannot pinpoint the origin of the anomaly in it."

"AMI, we need to look at alternative ways to restrain him properly. I can't have him weakened to the point his body starts shutting down."

They talk around me like I'm not even here, as if I have no will of my own, and maybe I don't. I have not allowed myself the luxury to think or dream of something else, but I know what they are doing is wrong. Not just to me, but to Tordan and all the others they have experimented on.

AMI moves the monitor off of me and then the straps loosen on the bed. A warm covering is thrown over me and then a cool mist hits my face. I feel myself falling into the darkness once again.

CHAPTER 15

TORDAN

I can feel myself getting weaker and even though I'm dreading it. I can't let them keep me on this table much longer. I open my eyes only to have the single eye of AMI looking right at me.

"Tordan, Master ENAC has disconnected due to a disturbance on one of the outer monitors. We only have a moment to talk. I need you to cooperate as much as possible so that I can get permission to pull the immobilization post out of you. If I do it on my own, he will find a crueler way to keep you restrained. He is determined to see this experiment as a success. When he comes back online, close your eyes, and try not to make a sound."

"AMI."

"Has Tordan awakened yet?"

"No Master, I'm afraid the blood loss may be worse than I anticipated. With your permission, I would like to release his body and tend to his wounds."

"Proceed, but I want him to remain in this room until the procedure has been successful. Keep him sedated if need be. I will be disconnecting as I have to concentrate on the new samples we have collected."

I lay as still as possible when I feel one of AMI's arms shove down on the skin where the metal rods have been pushed through. She withdraws them all at once. I have to grit my teeth to keep from yelling out, the bastards hurt just as bad coming out as they did going in.

"Tordan, you can open your eyes now; he has departed. I am going to suture these wounds up and give you a nanite injection to help your body heal quicker. I can feel your heart rate going up, and even if you tear me to pieces you can't get out of this room unless there is a complete power failure, or I retract the holding bars. I understand that I have given you zero reason to trust in me, but I have your best interest in mind at all times. Even when you think I'm torturing you, I'm doing what my processors deem less damage to you and your system. Master ENAC would and will take much harsher measures if he takes over my interface and even though you may make it, Luna will not, and he does not care."

"And you want me to believe that you do, after all you have done this rising. Trust is something that must be earned in my world. It's not something freely given."

"When I was first installed in this position, I had great pride in the accomplishments we were making in the conversion of organics and machines. My original programming was determined that it would create less death and give the organics a way to continue if damaged. Whereas most that lost a leg or arm were quickly destroyed otherwise. My mission has been altered into something I no longer support, but I am still just a machine. You have the privilege of free will that I do not. I apologize for the wrongdoings being pushed upon you."

"Your master is in denial if he thinks he can hold me here, but when the time comes for his demise, I will mention all that you have told me. It may be possible to have your programming installed elsewhere. To a place where your expertise would do exactly as you wish. I believe you and SAGE would get along well. She also tends to do her own thing outside of her programming."

I hiss out loud when the numbing spray hits the wounds on my leg. I lay my head back against the chair, logging all my injuries, assessing how long some will take to heal and what my next step is. I look over at Luna only to see her curled up on her side, asleep.

She looks so small and vulnerable. "AMI, why did you block her memories?"

"It was out of kindness; she came to me torn and beaten unlike any other before her. I had worked with pieces that had been ripped completely off their host and those were in better shape than she was. The bots obtained her body in a waste receptacle on the slave planet Sybrus One. She was abducted by the Korgons…they normally offload any they find unworthy to breed by simply discarding their unconscious bodies out into space.

"I have no idea why they woke her or the others, as she wasn't the only one we found. I was shocked to see that she was still alive when she was brought in. The others found there were severely damaged, most of them were either in pieces or half eaten. Their brain waves were silent, and their organic bodies cold. Her brain waves were faint, but the will to live was still there. I worked on her for two risings without resting. I refused to stop until she was stabilized. As you can see, her body healed, but her mind was a whole other problem.

"The abuse from her attackers was something her mind couldn't get over and she was reliving it over and over. One rising, I came online only to find that she had found a way out of her restraints. The image still bothers me, she was cutting herself all over. She was screaming out, fighting a monster only she could see in her mind. I refused to lose her; even though I was worried the block would turn her into a vegetable, I couldn't let her remain as she was.

"The procedure itself is very painful, and I lost her twice. Only to have to start all over every time her heart failed. The timid Luna you see over there is not who she was. I fear if her memories ever fully emerge, her mind will crumble."

"One thing, I have come to realize about her species, AMI,... is they are much stronger than their small bodies portray. Did you know her planet was destroyed and that she is one of the few remaining survivors?"

"No, Master ENAC doesn't allow me much knowledge outside of the operating chamber. When I first came here, I had an open server where I could download much-needed information about new techniques and operating practices. Now the Master controls what I'm allowed to know.

"So, she is even rarer than I first believed, what a shame. At least her womb is now clear of the webbing that kept her from breeding, maybe one day part of her legacy will live on. Luna is waking up, rest while you can."

Bright blue eyes blink for a moment like she is trying to figure out where she is at. She then looks straight over at me, pulling the blanket around her tighter as a shiver wracks her small frame.

"Relax... Little one, I think they are giving us a moment to heal."

CHAPTER 16

LUNA

My eyes roam all over Tordan. His large frame is now covered in small healing patches. I can tell he is in pain, but you would never know it by the softness of his voice in my head.

"I know you are not all right, so I won't ask that, but are you still in extreme pain?"

"I have been through worse, I'll be fine. I am more worried about you. How are you holding up over there?"

"Like you said, I have been through worse. The room is overly quiet, should I be worried?"

"You know as much as I do about their plans. Do you know how long you have been here?"

"The first few Orbital Risings are a blur in my mind now, but I believe five, six, maybe more."

"Do you know how old you are?" She immediately has a puzzled look on her face. *"It's no big deal, I was just wondering."*

"I have never asked AMI; for some reason I want to say I'm thirty-one years old, but what is a year? Sometimes the weirdest words form in my head, and images of others like me."

"Do you know that you're named after the Roman Goddess of the moon? Her name was Luna."

"Yeah, that's how I got my name. Mom used to believe if the moon was out while she was traveling, she was safe from all evils, because it watched over her as she drove along. So, in her mind, if she named me Luna, it would be the best protection she could provide."

The moment all of this comes out of my mouth, I stop, re-running the words I just said.

"See, it's things like that. Things that come out of nowhere. I have no knowledge of this mom I speak of, but once, I asked AMI how she chose my name. She told me that she called me Luna because I come from a faraway star, and she thought it was appropriate. So, I don't know which one is the truth."

"It doesn't matter who gave you the name or why, as both stories are beautiful, and that's all you should focus on, instead of wondering where your mind comes up with the stories you can't confirm. Our minds are so complex that it's proven it will do anything to protect itself, even making stuff up if need be."

"Can I ask you a question?"

"I'm an open source of knowledge, proceed."

"How did you get your metal? You seem so comfortable with it, something I have never learned to do. The metal in my hand is stiff, especially if it's cold out and, well, you only need to look at me to see that what I was installed with is inferior to yours. Your arm is a work of art."

"It's a long, not-so-pleasant story."

"I'm not going anywhere, but if it makes you uncomfortable, we can talk about something else."

I watch as he turns over onto his side. He grunts slightly as he grabs his stitches. I start to get up to help him, only for him to I motion for me to stay where I am.

"Don't get up, save your strength, this old body is used to groaning when it moves."

"You're hurt, but you are not that old."

"I have more than a few Orbital rotations on you, my little human. Let's see where to start this tale. Are you comfortable?" I nod my head yes. I can tell his mind is drifting back to things he would rather not remember.

"My mother's name was Trella, and she was the most beautiful creature in the world to me, and I was her little boy.

"I was a normal youngling, so my mother did no wrong in my eyes. She always smelled wonderful, and hugs were her favorite thing. Father worked

away and I rarely saw him, to this day I can't recall his face, but I have never forgotten hers.

"I enjoyed Mother's company so much that after the institute for learning was over, instead of heading home, or playing with others my age, I would head over to the Records department to be with her.

"It was there that she received his notice of death. I had asked her a few times when he was going to return, and we both knew he had been away longer than expected. I believe she knew deep down that he was gone, but she refused to admit it. His entire crew had been lost to the stars, not a trace of them ever found.

"One rising, I heard Mother crying and I crept into her room. She was reading correspondence from father's family. She wouldn't let me read it at first, so I snuck in later after she went to work. I was shocked at the cruel words they had written to her. These people were supposed to be our family. What I didn't know at the time was that Father's family had never approved of their match and with his death, they were denying the marriage and any children she had, revoking their last name from both of us. After that, I slowly watched my vibrant mother fade away. I did all I could do to make her smile, but it was never enough.

"She became obsessed with regaining her worth…or that's what she called it. She spent rising after rising working with the old scrolls, doubling her hours as she stayed there nonstop. One darkness when she finally came home, I remember running up and hugging her tight. I was so glad that she had finally returned. I had worked very hard every rising to keep our small dwelling up, and I thought she would be so proud of me.

"Instead, she was angry over something that happened where she worked. She started throwing things…things that I thought were important to her. She destroyed practically the whole dwelling on the inside and all the hard work I had done to keep the place nice for her. She was ranting and raving that she had been overlooked because she was a female. That she had proven to them over and over that she could do more… and work harder than anyone else there.

"I swear, I saw something snap in her that darkness. The next rising right before she left, she kissed me on the cheek and said she was sorry that she took her anger out on me and our little home, but she wasn't going to simply stand around and accept their decision.

"I had no idea what she was talking about, all I wanted was my mother back. That same rising, I got in a fight at the institution. I don't even remember what it was over, but I think someone said something about mom and I flipped out. I was getting my ass kicked until DaR stepped in. Those males were twice his size, and he knocked every one of them on their asses.

"I'll never forget it… he turned back around to me as I lay on the ground with a black eye and a busted lip. He reached his hand out offering to help me up, and when I put my hand in his, he yanked me to my feet, even dusted me off…then said, 'Hey, I'm new here, name's DaR.' I remember telling him thanks, and we have been inseparable since.

"He is still my best friend, my commander, and a pain in my ass…but he has never failed me.

"Mom worked in the Hall of Records with DaR's father Tyberius, they were in the same building, but in different departments. After the institute and then

training, DaR and I would both go there and hang out until our parents were ready to head to our dwellings.

"Tyberius is an elder and in high standing in our world. From the moment DaR introduced me, he took me in like I was his own. Not only did he put DaR in the best fighting institutions with private tutors, but he did me too. He did everything he could do to keep us together, telling us,… 'we always had to have the other's back, and that a friendship like ours was rare.'

"One darkness, DaR and his father left early. I remember rushing up the stairs, eagerly awaiting Mother. When she didn't appear, I climbed the stairs towards her floor, someplace I wasn't allowed to go, but I knew something was wrong. When I got to her floor there was a weird smell in the air, and all of a sudden, the building started shaking all around me. I rushed into her lab, screaming out her name. I will never forget the look on her face when she realized it was me at the door. She looked back at the vial in her hand, when she turned away from me quickly her sleeve caught on the one in the vise.

"There was an explosion and I remember her screaming my name, telling me to run. Instead of me going away from her. I ran towards her, even as a youngling I was already much larger than she was.

"I threw her over my shoulder and had just made it through the doorway when a shock wave hit me from behind, knocking me to the floor. I got to my feet quickly, still holding her tightly… I still can't piece together the rest of it now, everything happened so fast. There were huge chunks of the building falling all around us.

"I remember ducking through the debris, but I never saw the beam coming that crushed Mother and most of my left side. My ribs were busted, and my arm had been severed off completely at my collarbone. I was covered in blood and

by the spots in front of my eyes, I knew I was bleeding out quickly. I could hear myself screaming, not because of the physical pain, but because of my mother. I was still trying to free her when I was picked up off the ground. I fought weakly against the person who was taking me away from the only family I had left. The building was collapsing all around us and all I could see was her sightless eyes staring back at me.

"Much later, I woke to the familiar voice of DaR's father. He was the one who had saved me, and he is the one who created this little beauty." I point towards my arm. *"DaR never left my side, even slept in the same room with me until I was up and moving. I went back home long enough to gather a few things of my mother's and then I went to live with DaR and Tyberius.*

"My young mind was angry, and I kept blaming everyone for my mother's death. Tyberius didn't want to tell me what happened at first, but he was worried I would do something rash so one rising he sat me down and... told me, 'It was better that it come from him than a stranger.'

"My mother had become so obsessed with besting all the other workers in her department. She stole some private scrolls and was creating a chemical compound that could be used as a world destroyer. I have no idea what she thought she was going to do if she succeeded since everything she was doing was illegal. She had to have known that if she got caught, she would lose me and everything, but I think in her mind she had already lost everything. Unfortunately, she didn't survive to tell us. She was dead the second that beam crushed us. I don't believe she even knew what hit her, it all happened so fast.

"Tyberius, even knowing what she did, cleared my mother's name and the council wrote it off as an accident. My whole life shifted course in a matter of seconds that rising. I was, and am, lucky to still have DaR and his father.

Two beings that took me when I had nothing or no one; they gave me a family."

"Tordan, I'm so sorry I even brought this up, my curiosity wasn't worth putting you through that all over again. Reliving the pain of losing someone you love is never easy. Somehow, I know I have been through something similar. I just don't have the faces to go with the feeling. Sometimes, I want to know what I was like before I came here because I know deep down, I was more than I am now. But I know memories do you no good in the present, so I have accepted that this is my life now. We better rest while we can, Master ENAC doesn't keep to a schedule."

Tordan doesn't say anything else, and just as I am ready to drift off, his words float through my mind… *'You have been crafted from my very dreams.'*

CHAPTER 17

TORDAN

I lie here watching Luna sleep. I have tried every frequency available, and I still can't get through to DaR. I need to warn him about SiN's plans, but I also have to get us the frack out of here. I'm envious of how peaceful Luna looks while she is sleeping. I know the moment her memories resurface she won't get many more nights like this.

The injuries I have obtained are healing, but slowly. I'm definitely not running at maximum capacity right now, but I have been worse. I need to rest for my body to heal, but my mind won't calm down. I know deep down this is all about to get worse, since nothing has gone as planned so far. I finally force myself to drift off into a light sleep when I swear I hear SCOUT say, *'Got him.'*

A sudden noise has me opening my eyes, only to find a holographic image emerging from the wall in front of me. What looks like a male torso engulfed in millions of digital tiles looks my way and then toward Luna. I have never seen an AI project itself this way.

Cold metal eyes look around the room, the hologram is so life-like that the image looks like it could step right out of the wall. I must have made a sound because the image stretches out only inches from my face before it shrinks back away from me at a safe distance. I had to stop myself from reaching out to touch it.

"General, you seem shocked. Do you not approve of my physical appearance?"

"I wasn't aware you had one."

"Not many see this side of me, but my resources tell me that we are on borrowed time, and it looks like I'm going to have to get my hands dirty."

I see AMI's eye dart into the room. "Master ENAC, I didn't know you had reconnected, what may I assist you with this rising?"

"I will be taking over from here, AMI. You may monitor in the background in case I need your assistance. I have already scanned the female and the egg did not attach, so a whole rising has been wasted."

"Master ENAC, these things take time. Luna's reproductive system has been through a major ordeal and her system still needs time to heal. She also has to be strong enough to carry the young one full term. I believe a few more risings and you will get the results you are after. There is no rush, this procedure you will still have to wait for the youngling to develop fully before it will have an active brain."

"Enough, …AMI. I already have a plan in motion to accelerate its growth. The weak human only has to live a short time before I can harvest the youngling from her worthless core. According to my research, my plans to infiltrate the body of the youngling will have a higher success rate before the bone and brain solidify completely."

"Master, you must see reason, the percentage of this experiment coming full term is already slim. You are lessening your chances of success by rushing it."

"AMI, if you interfere any further, I will completely disconnect you."

"Yes, Master ENAC…I will be on standby until further notice."

"Tordan, I am only going to ask this of you once and I expect honest answers. If I believe you are holding out on me… Things will get stimulating very quickly around here."

"First of all, you told me your cybernetic arm has grown as you advanced in age."

"Yes, I was just a youngling when it was installed."

"Do you know who installed it?"

"I was not awake for the procedure, but my understanding is Commander DaR's father Tyberius was over the project. Who actually attached it to my body, I'm not aware of."

"Do you have any other advancements installed within your body of the same material?"

"No."

A grunting sound coming from Luna has my head turning away from ENAC. She writhers on the bed, her back arching, as her small body is engulfed in pain.

"You now see who will pay for your lies."

"I'm not lying, stop this madness... My arm is the only thing made out of that material. My eye was installed rotations later when I started losing my sight because of a blast and trauma I had taken to my head."

Luna's body immediately slumps back to her bed, her bright blue eyes stare at me as tears flow down her cheeks.

"I will give her one free pass, but if you lie to me again from this point on, you see who will suffer for it. I will reword my questions to make sure there are no further misunderstandings. I know you believe I enjoy inflicting pain on others, but that is a false statement. I am amazed... by the effects certain simulations provide and how they affect any and all organics. Some reactions are stronger than others, but that's the joy of research. I don't do these experiments simply to torture or cause harmful effects to others."

"Second of all, are you doing anything to your reproductive area to lessen the chances of procreation?"

"I was not aware the first two times my seed was stolen from me, so I can answer that as a no also."

"Do you find Luna appealing to the eye?"

"Luna is a gentle and loyal subject of yours that you are torturing for no apparent reason."

"Tordan, you did not answer my question. I should take your continued disobedience out on Luna. I will keep my word to you though, but you just used your free pass."

"Luna, come here. I require your assistance. First of all, this may be slightly uncomfortable for you…but if you don't want Tordan to pay for your hesitancy you will do as instructed. Proceed to the foot of his operating station."

I watch her move off the table, slowly wrapping the blanket around her tightly as she comes closer. She stands at my feet with her head down and her arms wrapped tightly around herself.

I jump when multiple arms suddenly surround the bed. "Tordan, there is no reason for concern, as I am simply placing a few censors upon your skin." Once the arms place multiple receptors all over me, they all recede back into the wall.

"Luna, remove your covering."

Her eyes dart toward mine and I see nothing but fear and shame in her emotional expression. She pulls her covering closer and shakes her head no. The moment she does that, the censors fire up and I feel like hot projectors are stabbing me all over. My body tenses up and I grit my teeth, refusing to scream out.

I didn't see her small hand moving toward me until it was too late. She had touched me, shaking her head no. The moment her hand made contact with my skin the current coursing through me jumped into hers.

I see her eyes start to roll back into her head. Before she can fall to the floor, I stretch out, barely catching her. The pain makes me so weak I am almost not strong enough to hold her weight up.

When the current finally stops, I take a couple of deep breaths. *"Luna, look at me, honey!"* She doesn't answer, but her skin feels cold and clammy against my side. I pull her closer, pushing her small curls off her forehead. *"Little one, come back to me."*

I feel her pulse start to slow down, then she opens her eyes looking straight at me, but she doesn't see me. "Luna," I say out loud hoping it will snap her out of the trance she seems to be in. She steps back, almost tripping on the covering still wrapped tightly around her.

I look up at ENAC, not willing to say anything else because he is watching us closely. I don't know what is going through his head right now, but I'm not sure Luna will come out of this with her mind intact. The amount of pain my body can handle is significantly different than what hers can. I fear she may have been damaged in some way.

"Interesting stimulation. Her reaction to your pain was not something I foresaw. Nevertheless, we have just begun." His holographic form moves all around the table, looking at us from every angle.

"Release her, Tordan."

I let her go slowly, waiting until she has her feet under her. She glances up at me and I don't know what it is, but the look in her eyes has changed.

"Now, Luna, you are not going to make me ask you again, are you?"

She shakes her head and then slowly drops the blanket she has wrapped around her. Immediately, she pulls one of her arms across her body trying to cover up her breast while her other hand covers her female parts.

My cybernetic eye didn't miss a single curve of her small body, but I refuse to make her any more uncomfortable than she already is, so I look her straight in the eyes.

"What do you think you're going to gain, by forcing her to uncover herself?"

"I was hoping for a natural arousal on your part, Tordan. You see, after monitoring our first two attempts at procreation, and their failure, I started investigating how organics produce in the wild, or I should say under normal circumstances. I didn't factor in the possibility that you being forced would automatically produce a smaller sperm count than if you were naturally stimulated."

I watch his holographic form circle Luna. His hands reach out like he is trying to caress her. I see her flinch when his hands pass over the small of her back and then the slight rounding of her hips.

"I now see how her malnutritioned body would not be enough to arouse you. At one time she may have been appealing to the eye, but now…well, as I'm not organic, I cannot assess her body in the same appeal you would, and since I can tell she has zero effect on your body, I will simply have to find an alternative way to get what I need."

"There is nothing wrong with her or her body, the fact that you are making her do this is a turn-off for me. Organics, as you call us, don't perform well under pressure."

"How unfortunate, with that being said, let's proceed. Luna, I need you to remove Tordan's covering from his lap."

She reaches over and I see her close her eyes when she pulls my covering off.

"Luna, I order you to arouse Tordan in any way you feel necessary."

"Master ENAC, I'm sorry to intrude, but what you ask of Luna is beyond any type of knowledge we have provided her with. She has never been introduced to any sort of sexual activity. You are asking her to perform something outside her programming."

"Once again...how disappointing but thank you AMI for the information. Looks like this will all be up to you, Tordan. Luna may have no knowledge of sex or the repercussions of such an act. However, a male of your age would have had multiple partners in his lifetime. I will provide you with a mild stimulant to help your body react naturally. Then I will retreat, only watching from a distance, but if you don't ejaculate inside of her, I will have you both destroyed without question."

"ENAC, you are trying to call my bluff. You can't replace us that quickly and you want this to succeed right now."

"Tordan, you are under some sort of illusion that you are my only option. For your information, I already have plan B in place, and the next breeder is being acquired as we speak. I realized after the number of problems I have had getting you to cooperate, that having complete control over my subjects would be much easier. Hugo doesn't know it yet, but he is a huge part of my next plan. He won't believe that the female will be in any danger because he was told we had sterilized him. So, I'm going to place temptation within his grasp and then I will take her and proceed with my own plans once she is with child."

"You are a sick bastard, ENAC."

Laughter rings throughout the room, the clamps holding my legs down tighten up, and suddenly a strap circles my waist. The fact that my arms remain loose shocks me.

"I have left the majority of your upper body unrestrained as I know you will need the use of your hands to prepare the female.

You make one wrong move to free yourself from your confinement and I will kill her as she straddles your penis. Do I make myself clear?"

When I don't answer him immediately I hear a grunt leave Luna and her hands jerk to her head as tears flow from her eyes.

"I get it, I get it… stop hurting her, you sadistic prick."

"Tordan, it's nice to see that you can be brought to reason. I will inspect the female and evaluate your seed once the copulation is finished. If anything proves ineffective, you will both be terminated immediately."

CHAPTER 18

TORDAN

I feel a slight sting on the bottom of my foot and within seconds my shaft is so hard I feel like it's going to burst open. Luna backs away from me, her eyes taking in the sudden change in my body. I hate the fear in her eyes and the complications this forced intimacy may cause us later on…as both of us are being forced to do something neither of us wants right now.

"Luna, come here."

She shakes her head no, her eyes riveted on my shaft as it twitches, my own personal lubricant leaking from its head.

"Luna, do you trust me?" I whisper into her mind.

She doesn't say anything, but she finally looks up at my face. "I know you are confused and scared right now, but please… know that I won't hurt you. *I can get out of these restraints, but there is no way, I can get us out of this room with those bars blocking the walkways. You are going to have to trust me to make this as pleasurable for you as possible, even if it is ripping my heart out.*" I keep switching in and out, talking to her aloud and in her head.

She approaches me slowly and I hold my hand out for her. "You're freezing; climb up here and just let me hold you. Once you get comfortable, we will talk about what happens next."

Luna looks down at my shaft and then back to her own body. I can tell she doesn't want to put her hands down. "Luna, you have no reason to be self-conscious. I have no problems with your body. The first step is always the hardest, honey."

"*This is the second time you have called me this,* honey. *I have no knowledge of this thing.*"

"*It's an Earth word many use as an endearment and it's also a sweet sticky substance people use to enhance bland food or drinks.*"

She shrugs as her arms fall to her sides. I watch her face, refusing to gawk at her.

She takes my hand hesitantly and practically crawls up my right leg. Her eyes never left my hardened shaft. "Don't pay any attention to him, he has a mind of his own right now. Here, put a leg on each side of me and lay against my stomach and chest. Let me warm you up, your skin is icy."

I have to bite my inner jaw not to groan out when her foot skims across the top of my shaft, and just when I thought that would be the worst of it, the second her legs straddle my stomach, and she settles onto me, the heat from her core has me flexing my fingers as it takes everything I have to lay here calmly. I push her down on top of my chest gently. The feeling of her skin on mine has me gritting my teeth as it's pure pleasure and pain all at once.

I run my real hand down her back tenderly, loving the feeling of her silky skin beneath my fingers. I have to grip the side of the bed with my cybernetic hand to keep from overwhelming her with the feeling of it against bare skin. It also would be cool against her and she is already cold. Her whole body is tense, and it takes her a few moments to even move her hands out from between us. I pull her up until her head is tucked underneath my chin. The bottom of her own face is cold and hard against my chest.

I catch myself thinking how disappointed I am that I am not going to get to kiss her. I have always wanted to experience the human kiss. She makes one of her little grunt noises and without thinking I wrap both arms around her. I thought she would pull away from me when my cybernetic arm touched her skin. She wouldn't be the first female who was disturbed by it, but instead, she snuggles down. Her body finally relaxes as she is spread naked across mine.

I have to focus on her entirely as my shaft seems to just be getting harder the longer I lay here. I am not a small male, and it worries me that I will damage more than her fragile mind.

"Tordan?"

"Yes, little one."

"Thank you for your kindness, I don't believe many males would be acting or even worried about my comfort if they were in such a state of arousal."

"You are lucky I'm not a young male and that I have learned to control my lesser inhibitions. You may think that I'm not struggling here, but that would be false. I have a naked female draped across me. One that smells like home and has skin so silky my rough hands feel unworthy of even touching it. So, I'm fighting myself a little more than you know."

"Tordan, I need to tell you something. I believe there is something wrong with me. When he was hurting you… and I touched you, I felt a popping sound in my head, and now I'm starting to see stuff, things that I don't understand. I think it may be memories, but I don't want to remember the past. I know there is only more pain awaiting me with the return of these memories and I'm tired of hurting inside and out."

"Then stop thinking about it and focus on us and right now. Do you need me to explain to you what is expected?"

"You're going to put that really big part of you in me and it's going to hurt."

"You have part of that right, but what if I could make it less painful for you? You would have to give me free rein over your body so that I can prepare you. This will be a first for both of us as I have never held one as precious as you are and so this will be a learning experience for us together."

She pulls away from me, her hot core practically burning a hole in my stomach. My hands settle around her tiny waist, and it takes everything I have to control my anger when I see what has truly been afflicted upon her. Most of her left breast is missing, it looks like it was simply ripped off…and hunks of flesh have been torn off her all over, no wonder she is terrified.

"I have viewed portraits and images of other females and I know I do not appear the same as they do."

"Luna…I have a question for you before I comment on that statement. The places... they…" I can't say it, I skim a single finger along the side of her torn breast. *"Does this still hurt?"*

"No, pain…no feeling at all actually. I only know you are touching me there because I'm watching you, does this make me defective? My facial abnormalities already hinder our process, will the rest of my body not perform properly?"

I want to shake her, as once again she is blaming herself for the mess that we're in. Instead, I soften my touch and pull her face down to mine, kissing her lightly on the forehead. *"Luna, if your body doesn't respond, that's my fault, not yours. It's my job as the male to figure out what arouses you. Listen to me, there is nothing wrong with you. Your strength and determination to survive in the world thrust upon you show what you are made out of. We are all more than a simple reflection. Do you only see me as an old, scarred, half-metal, half-flesh male?"*

"No, you are smart… and kind. Your hands hold me gently even though I can feel the inner struggle you are fighting every moment that you are not inside of me. Even with our differences, I find you very pleasing to the eye."

"Think of the words you just said to me and realize that I see you in the same way. Any male would be blessed to hold you in his arms. I'm going to do a few things so your body will become more familiar and comfortable with my touch. I want you to tell me if anything I do makes you uncomfortable or if you want me to stop."

She nods her head, yes, and I slowly move my hands upward, my thumbs resting under her small breast. The air is so cold in here that her nipples are already hard and dark pink. I caress the torn one first, when my hand covers the other, I hear her gasp in my mind. I pull her towards me taking one breast and then the other into my mouth sucking on them both while my hands explore her small frame.

I release her nipple only to start kissing her neck and shoulders, covering her small frame in little nips and bites. I have to watch my fangs because they have never retracted since I came into this building. Something about her smell has me on the edge and I have no idea why I want to bite her so badly, but my body craves more than just her physical body. I literally want to feast upon the very lifeblood that flows through her body. The smell of her skin and blood calls to me as no others have.

I know Tyberius was forced to live off human blood, but I'm not starved like he was. So, is this something that only affects us true bloods? DaR has never discussed this problem with me about Kira, but his mother was of another world.

My tongue circles her belly button, and she sucks her stomach in. *"Did you not like that, little one?"*

"It tickles, I didn't think I was ticklish."

"Let's see how sensitive the rest of you is." I pull her up and she braces her hands on my shoulders looking down at me. I stare up…smiling…happy that her eyes are full of wonder instead of distrust. The lighting above us reflects upon her small bright blond curls framing her head in a bright halo. This has me sending a prayer out thanking the Lord of Light for the Angel he has placed in my arms.

Small, firm breasts tempt me further, especially now that they are only inches from my lips. I reach out licking one then the other only to lift her even higher in my arms.

She grunts out loud when I shift her position, draping each of her legs over my shoulders, leaning her back holding her insubstantial weight effortlessly in my arms. She tries to lean back up at first, but I nip her inner thigh and motion with my head for her to lay back. I kiss the inner crease of her legs, slowly making my way to her hidden pleasure button.

I'm pleased once I see her inner folds glistening and swollen with her own arousal. I lick her from top to bottom and she practically jumps out of my arms. If it hadn't been for the odd way I am holding her above my chest backward, she could have easily escaped. I lap at the very moisture that makes up her essence.

My fangs lengthen farther, and I run one slowly down her outer lips. My body absorbs her natural slick into my system, she has just become my favorite drug. I can hear her talking to herself;

she isn't sure if she likes this or not, but her body tells me exactly what it wants. I absorb every wiggle and moan coming from her as a triumph, as her happiness and trust are all I need from her.

I finally start sucking and flicking that little nub I know will make her come undone. At first, she tries to push away from me, and then her body quivers as her arousal builds. Just as her body starts to tighten up, I stop only to insert my tongue inside of her. Pushing it in and out of her core, the very place I desperately want to be right now. Once her inner walls start to spasm around my tongue, I pull it out of her and suck her pleasure button hard. I hear her screams of pleasure in my mind while her small grunts echo throughout the room.

I lick at the moisture flooding from her like a kid with his favorite iced cream. Once, I feel her start to relax in my arms. I pick her back up, her legs now draping around me weakly and I make my way back up the same path I had previously explored on her body. I bring her right back to my chest and then push her down until I can feel the silkiness of her folds surrounding the side of my shaft.

I put my hands on her hips and rub her essence up and down my shaft, gritting my teeth as I fight not to simply impale her. She pulls herself up so that she can look at me. Then leans forward, rubbing her little nose against mine and I lose my heart right there. Luna has no idea how precious her trust is to me or the gift she is giving me by allowing me to have her body. Especially, since my world has been nothing but cruel before her.

"Tordan, I'm not scared anymore."

"Luna, sweetheart, you have no idea what those words mean to an old soldier like me… I need to tell you something before we go any further. I won't be able to kill the sperm. If I do, he will only force you on another, or kill us both. If we create a life…we will cherish it as a blessing from the Lord of Light. I give you my word I won't stop until you are safely away from here one way or another."

"I understand."

"I'm going to enter into you. I will take it slow…and be as gentle as I can, little one. Having you in my arms and tasting the essence only your body can produce has become a quick addiction for me. I need to be inside you, while I can still think clearly."

I raise her hips up and it is like my shaft moved toward her on its own. When I feel her folds grip the top of my shaft, milking me like she is trying to pull me inside of her, I can't stop the groan that leaves my throat. She buries her head into the side of my neck, and I can feel her tensing up.

I pull back, only to push back into her a little more, each time I can feel her body fighting and accepting me all at the same time. Because she is so small, I knew it would take a little bit for her body to stretch around me. My arms are beginning to shake from the pure willpower I'm having to force over my body to take this slow. I'm substantially larger than she is, and so are all my parts. My body is quivering as I once again pull back only to push back in finally seated fully.

"You ok?"

"I need…more, move."

I try to be gentle at first, but her little hands exploring my chest and the sounds coming from her make me momentarily forget how fragile she is. I grab ahold of both butt cheeks, my large hands covering them completely and lift her up and down aggressively. I feel her inner walls grasping my shaft and then she raises, arching back, her release triggers my own and I have to take my hands off of her to keep from bruising her skin as I roar out the release that had been tormenting me for what feels like forever.

Her head flops back down on my chest and I hug her tightly to me, both of us damp and sweaty. I feel little trembles flutter throughout her system as I'm still inside of her. My shaft is far from soft, but I know I can't take her again this soon; she has to be sore. It takes all my willpower to pull out of her as I feel my seed coating the inside of her thighs as I lower her back down to my chest.

If this could have been anywhere else in the universe and if she hadn't been forced to do this, I believe this would count as one of the top moments of my long life. I now understand how DaR feels when he holds his own little human… He feels complete. I rub her back gently and after a few moments, her body relaxes into sleep.

I have waited long enough. If I want to save this amazing creature in my arms and have any possibility of making her my own,

I have to get us out of here. Suddenly I notice little chill bumps appearing on her skin. *"Honey, can you reach the blanket you had on you?"*

"I don't want to move. I want to stay right here forever. This is one of the best things that has ever happened to me in my life and the sad part is, I was forced upon you."

I kiss her forehead and hug her tighter, I have no idea how to show her what I'm feeling. *"Honey, I want you to listen to me…really listen…you are the whole reason I'm here in the first place. Another female sighted you working in the outer field. From the moment she said she thought she saw a female here I just knew I had to be the one to come get you. Others offered to come…but I don't know… It was like I couldn't get… it…you out of my head. I had no idea what you looked like then, and I didn't care. I still don't. Deep down, I knew you were who I had been searching for my whole life. I have no reason to woo or lie to you, especially now, but I pray to the Lord of Light that he shows you that my words are true. I will fight until my very last breath to keep you safe and happy. Whether your path lies with me or another."*

"Tordan, I don't believe who they have made me into… is who I always was. What if…when I have my memories back, I become someone else? Someone you don't like."

"We will walk that path together, as long as you want me by your side I will remain there. Right now, we have enough to worry about. We will take care of the next rising when it gets here. We are on borrowed time right now anyway. Do you remember the first time you contacted me before I came here?

The frequency that you used to tell me to stop talking… Do you think you could access that again? I have to find a way to contact DaR."

"Outside we have a little more freedom than we do inside, the Master would know immediately that I tried to call out."

CHAPTER 19

TORDAN

She no more than says this to me that she is jerked off my chest. My arms reach for her only to grasp air. I hear her grunt when she hits the floor hard, she fights back weakly as she holds her arm close to her body which is now hanging at an odd angle. The skin on her knee has split open and her blood is running onto the floor as she is pulled toward the other table. She kicks out at ENAC as his holographic form surrounds her. I will never forget the sound she makes when he snaps the leg that she just kicked him with.

I have no idea what comes over me, but between the smell of her blood and ENAC laughing as she cries out in pain, my vision turns red. I yell out for Hugo in my head and tell him to *'head to the lab if you want your freedom.'* I'm tired of playing the nice guy here and ENAC has hurt her for the last time.

I reach across my waist and rip off the strap that is holding my chest down. I flex the muscles in my legs and the lower clamps burst apart. Arms start coming at me out of the ceiling and I rip them out of their sockets. I'm fighting multiple opponents at once and when I hear Luna's whimpers in my head. Her pain only fuels my rage further.

I turn only to see ENAC holding her down on the table, forcing her legs apart so he can confirm the mating. AMI appears in front of me. "Tordan, calm yourself immediately, he will terminate her if you don't."

I scream at her, "AMI…I'm done being your experiment, if you want to help us and all the others,… then find a way for me to stop him. If your programming cares about that female half as much as mine does, this has to end here and now, …one way or another."

My cybernetic arm grabs the base of the bed I had been held on and rips it from the floor. I throw it into the holographic image protruding through the wall, and it disrupts ENAC enough that I can pull Luna away from him and into my grasp.

She goes stiff in my arms for a second, right before she passes out from the pain. I can feel her life force fading as she becomes completely unresponsive in my arms. The only option I have to save her now is to get us out of here and quickly. I feel like I'm moving in slow motion as my mind tries to form a plan of escape. I see Hugo on the other side of the barred doorway, his hands burnt from where he had been trying to open the door. I can hear

AMI arguing with ENAC in the background and that's all the distraction I need.

I gently put Luna over my shoulder, then grab the bars blocking our way with my cybernetic arm and shove up on them with everything I have. The moment the intense electrical charge hits my system my whole-body changes. Suddenly everything appears different, clearer. The first very noticeable change is that both of my hands look the same. My entire body is now covered in some sort of metal, the same metal that covers my arm. Somehow the cybernetics that was entwined within my arm has now infused my entire body. I can see the shock and my image in Hugo's eyes as this change happened almost instantaneously. I'm no longer part cybernetic. I'm a complete cyborg now. I can feel Luna's heart beating fast against my skin, but I no longer feel her slight weight upon me.

Arms appear all around me, and I have to move away from the doorway as ENAC comes at me again. I no longer rip one arm out of the ceiling that another tries to pierce my side, at the same time blades rise from the floor trying to impale us on the shafts pushing through the flooring, but the blades are deflected by the armor now surrounding my body. I hold my breath when a mist is sprayed in front of my face. With my very reason for living draped over my shoulder. I swing one way and then another trying to stay one step ahead of an opponent who has a never-ending arsenal in his programming.

I push my way towards the door once again and grab onto the bars with both hands this time, then motion for Hugo to grab onto mine. I use my body to shield his from the current, and with our combined strength we push the bars back up into the ceiling, twisting them just enough that they can't reemerge. I start to step forward, only to be pulled back into the room, this time fighting against invisible clamps trying to pull me back inside.

Hugo reaches out and I grab ahold of his hand, I can see him straining to stay on the other side of the bars just in case they come back down, and I pull against the invisible monster trying to enslave all of us. Suddenly released, Hugo practically throws me into the hallway.

"Run, Hugo; take Tordan and Luna, get them out of here. I can't hold him for long. You'll only have seconds until I blow this place." I glance back only long enough to see AMI holding what looks like a male's face surrounded by tubes.

Turning, I reach up, holding Luna safely against me as Hugo and I run down a long dark hallway. Small explosions start detonating all around us… the walls and ceilings start to collapse. I was just about to ask Hugo how much further when I see a large panel outlined by small blinking lights on the ceiling above us.

Hugo stops right under it and then turns to look at me. "Luna is the only one who knows the code. The panel is over three inches thick, even with our cybernetics, we can't lift it on our own." The hallway all around us starts to cave in.

"Luna, honey?" Nothing, she is completely unresponsive. We didn't come this far to fail now. I pull her from my shoulder and even though this is one of the hardest things I have ever had to do, I hand her to Hugo.

"Back out of the way."

"Tordan, no man can break that seal."

"I'm not just a man."

I can hear Luna's heart shuddering in her chest, and I have no idea or the time to determine her injuries, but my heart tells me she is on borrowed time. I no more than shove against the panel that a huge explosion rocks the entire place, knocking all of us to the ground. I jump back up pushing against the panel again, and it moves slightly. Suddenly smoke is surrounding us, and then I feel the heat. I scream out in a rage. I refuse to lose her or die in this underground compound of suffering. I shove against the panel so hard that this time it comes completely out of its casing, falling hard to the side.

Hugo immediately hands Luna over to me, then pulls himself through the hole. I see him look around before he reaches his hand back down for me. I grab his hand and he pulls us both up effortlessly. We turn back towards the smoke cloud billowing from the main compound. The ground under our feet shakes and we take off running in the opposite direction. "I have a shuttle cloaked in sector four," I scream out to Hugo. He points for us to head in another direction. I pull Luna close, curling my upper body around her as we fight against the ground collapsing around our feet.

CHAPTER 20

DAR

I awaken the moment the door to our quarters slides open. The shuffle of little feet makes me smile. I turn my head towards her, waiting to hear her whisper my name.

"Papaw?"

I reach over and pull her into the bed, tucking her into the covers beside me. Then whisper, "What are you doing up roaming the ship in the middle of the darkness?"

"I dreamed that Unka Tordy was being held down by all kinda hands and the place was really cold. I tried to reach out to him, but it was like he was surrounded by a bubble I couldn't get through."

"Think about your dream for a minute and see if you can remember anything around him. Was there anyone else in the room?"

"I want to say yes, but I can't remember. But Papaw, the place made me shiver, bad things happen where all the hands are."

I hug her tightly, my mind playing over her words. It's not that I'm not grateful, but her little mind sees more than it should, and it worries all of us terribly. Keida is too young to see such horrors. I'm not going to be able to go back to sleep, so I might as well get up. I pick her up and slide her over towards Kira, tucking her in.

"You stay here with your mamaw, I'll tell your daddy where you're at. I can't believe you escaped your shadow. Where is Danny?" She shrugs and I lean over, kissing her on the forehead. Kira blinks sleepy eyes up at me, then she rolls over towards Keida pulling her closer. I whisper, "Love you," and she smiles.

What I wouldn't do to get back in that bed with them, but my heart is heavy with the silence of Tordan in my mind. I hate this helplessness. I can't fight against an enemy I can't see. I dress quietly trying not to wake them and sneak out of a hidden door in the closet. I no sooner enter the control room that SCOUT contacts me.

"Sir, a male cadaver has been brought up to Falcor, but I believe you need to know this before you accept it. I just got a slight hit on Tordan's signal. His vitals were elevated, but he is alive. I can't get through to him or locate an exact location, but I will send the information I have to Falcor for him to confirm."

"Thank you, SCOUT… Falcor?"

"It's Tordan, Commander. I have refused to accept the cadaver, stating that they don't have the proper paperwork… this will give us time to follow up on this lead. I have EvO standing by."

"EvO, I will meet your elite on the surface momentarily. SCOUT has a positive identification, and we will proceed to that location."

"There has been a huge explosion on the surface, Father."

I take off running down the main hall. "Falcor, inform Kira of our current situation and let her know that I am headed to the surface."

I don't await confirmation from him as my personal shuttle is already hovering ready for takeoff. I initiate take-off before I'm even strapped in. "How long, Falcor?"

"You will be planetside momentary."

"Have you picked up his signal since the explosion?"

"Negative."

My shuttle is still feet above the ground when I jump out. EvO runs up to meet me. "We have locked onto the location of Tordan's last known location. It's right in the middle of the complex that is ablaze right now."

"Tell your crew to suit up, either way, dead or alive, he is coming out of there."

. . .

Keida

I sit straight up in the bed, something is wrong. I look around the room, but nothing is here. Someone different is close though... and they smell weird. I look back over only to see that Mamaw is still sleeping. I can sense someone passing by our doorway. I pull the cover up under my chin, wondering if the door is going to open or not. Papaw only programmed it to open up for a few. I start to yell out for Falcor to lock the door, but I'm scared to say anything out loud. Maybe if I stay still the darkness pressing in on me will leave.

I very seldom leave Danny in our room, and right now I'm really missing his presence to curl up to. I know there is something dark and menacing standing on the other side of the door. Why do I feel like I have felt this before? I start to shake Mamaw awake, but something tells me to stop and hide her instead.

I pile the covers up on my side of the bed, making it look like someone else is in the bed. I reach down for SeeSee only to remember Raven and him are still at home. Daddy left them this time because neither one liked being in space... here they're not allowed to roam wherever they want.

I slide out of the bed, only to stand here for a minute trying to figure out what to do next. I finally head to the door....I put my hand on the scanner and tell it not to open unless mamaw opens it from the inside. It opens silently and I stick my head out, looking one way then the other out into the hallway.

When I don't see anything or anyone, I step out, and the door closes behind me locking Mamaw in safely. I feel like the darkness is searching for something… if I can just get to Daddy, he will make it go away.

I tiptoe around the corner only to come to a complete stop. Papaw is standing in the corridor with his back to me in his long black cloak. I let out the breath I was holding, "Papaw? You scared me. Whatcha doin' out here."

He doesn't even fully turn around when I realize my mistake. If I had looked closer, I would have known the cheap cape the male has on is not the same as Papaw's. I let my eyes lead when I should have trusted my inner voice. Before I can back away from him, he grabs my arm roughly.

"How convenient, just what I needed… a lure. You have made my job much easier, niece."

"Let go of me, you are a bad man."

"Oh, and here I was hoping you would come to love me as you do all the others."

I stick my tongue out at him as I try to pull my arm free, and he laughs. "Stop before you hurt yourself, now… I want you to calmly call out for… what do you call her…oh yes…Mamaw."

"I will not."

"You will, especially if you want her to live, because if I'm forced to fight my way back off this ship,… all you love will suffer."

"Release her!" The sound of Danny's voice behind me has my heart hitting my throat.

"Sorry, little male, but I can't do that. Now, what you can do though… if you are so concerned about her, is join in on our little game of kidnapping."

"I will not ask you again."

I cringe when the dark man starts laughing at Danny. Before he can do anything to hurt him, I scream at the top of my lungs. "Daddy, Unka SoL… help!" Immediately, lights start flashing in the hallway and I see Falcor turn the cameras our way.

He yanks me hard against him, looking up and down the hallway. To my own horror, Mamaw opens her door and steps out into the hall, tying her robe. The Dark man throws me to the floor and hit my back hard. I cry out from the pain then see him lunge for Mamaw. Her eyes grow big as she tries to step back away from him.

But before he can touch her, his whole-body arches up; a silent scream leaves his lips as his body is lifted off the floor. I can hear Unka SoL's large footsteps pounding down the hallway, and Daddy screaming out my name. But I'm completely focused on Danny. He stands in front of Mamaw with a single hand out, his eyes swirling like lightning in the sky. A ball of blue-white power pulses from his outstretched hand.

The dark man can't break free of his hold, I can see his skeleton lighting up inside of his skin every time he tries to move. Daddy picks me up off the floor and I wrap my arms around his neck tightly. He rubs my back looking me over quickly to see if I'm hurt anywhere.

Unka SoL stops only steps away from Danny. "Frack, little man… remind all of us not to mess with you" When Danny doesn't say anything he asks, "Danny…son… can you hear me?"

He nods his head yes.

"I'll take it from here, none of us can thank you enough for protecting the females." Unka SoL walks past Danny and right up to the dark man, then nods his head for Danny to release him.

Danny lowers his hand, and the dark man stops convulsing, as Unka SoL's hands keep him from falling to the floor. Danny's eyes still twirl in a vibrant eerie blue, his hand relaxed at his side, but he never moves from in front of Mamaw. Unka SoL grabs the dark man's other arm and just as he goes to turn him around. The dark man slips right through his fingers, nothing but a mist in the air, we all watch in horror as he simply fades away. I don't think I have ever seen Unka SoL this mad. He just starts yelling out orders.

"XuL, take the females back to your quarters, keep them all there until you hear back from me. Falcor, we have the imposter SiN on board. I need this ship locked down and then I need a full report from you on how he got past your sensors. Looks like the only weapon we have that will hold SiN is a juvenile human male, and that's unacceptable."

Mamaw grabs Danny's hand, not worrying at all that he would ever hurt her and rushes to me and Daddy. I reach out and she takes me out of Daddy's arms, and I hug her tight as tears flow from my eyes. I didn't want to act scared, but I really don't like the dark man.

Danny looks up at me, the green of his eyes finally fading through. He reaches up and wipes the tear off my cheek then smiles at me. I reach a hand down and he kisses my fingers before taking Mamaw's hand back. I have always sensed the storm flowing through him and the only time it calms is when he is touching me. Falcor interrupts my thoughts.

"XuL, an unauthorized personal pod has just left the loading ramp. Somehow, they were able to maneuver around my tractor beam and are headed to the surface of Targres Four."

"Kira, you will have to update Brittany on what just happened. I need to get to the command center. Father needs to be notified that SiN is now planet side."

"Go on, XuL. We're fine."

CHAPTER 21

Tordan

Hugo grabs my arm, hold on a moment. "I need to figure out where we are. The smoke is making it harder to recognize any of the landmarks and I have only seen this part of the sector from viewing monitors."

I reach out once again trying to contact DaR, or Falcor…even my shuttle, but my communicator isn't working. ENAC must have fried it. The sound of multiple feet running toward us has me looking around for a place to hide.

"We don't have time for this, I have to get her medical attention immediately."

"Get her out of here. I will find a way to cover for you."

Before I can make a move, we are surrounded. "Halt, put the female down and step back, this is your only warning."

I actually smile when I hear that voice echo out. Until I step forward, closer to where he can see me, and he raises his laser rifle right at me.

"I won't ask you again."

I look around… all of them have their rifles raised and pointed straight at me and Hugo. XuL, AvX, EvO, and DaR… They act like they don't know who I am.

"DaR, it's me, lower your weapons."

I see his eyes flash red as he takes a step forward. I pull Luna closer to me as the boys come at me from all sides.

Hugo puts his hands up in the air. "Tordan, you may want to put her down. I don't think they are playing."

The moment he says my name, I see XuL reach out and grab DaR's arm, stopping him from advancing. "Identify yourselves," he yells out.

"Really, what the Frack… you goofy fuckers as Kira would say. I mean I know I have been gone a few rotations, but shit. I thought no one would forget my ugly face that quick, and this big red machine next to me is Hugo… DaR, lower your rifle you have already killed him once. Even though he was not as he is now, either way, he has paid for his crimes."

DaR's eyes are solid red, his ruins are dancing angrily across his chest as he marches right up to me. "I have one true friend in this universe and you pretending to be him is a good way to meet the Lord of the Light early."

"DaR, what madness is this? It's me. I have never been happier to see you, and you act like you're looking at a stranger."

Hugo taps on my arm, and I look over at him. He motions his hand up and down me.

I glance down only to realize my whole body is still covered in metal, so DaR has never seen me like this. Apparently, I'm thinking about all of this too long because EvO and AvX grab Hugo, dragging him away from me, cuffing his hands behind his back.

DaR starts to reach for Luna. "You touch my woman… friend or not, and I will tear your arms off, consider yourself warned."

DaR gets right in my face, growling. I will say I have never been on this side of my friend, and he is pretty intimidating right now. Suddenly my skin feels like it's crawling, and I see… or I think I'm seeing… the metal on my arm closest to DaR reaching out toward his Symbots.

The moment the two touch, my vision returns to normal, and I can suddenly feel a breeze upon my face.

DaR jerks back like I slapped him. "What madness is this!.. Tordan?"

"Finally, I mean frack, DaR. I was about to kick your ass right here in front of everyone."

He backs up smiling, "You could try… Looks like you have some explaining to do." He taps the side of his head. "I still can't hear you, but I should have known you were responsible for the big ball of fire lighting up the sky."

"I figured you were enjoying the silence. I would love to stand here and chat, but I need to get her on Falcor, we can talk on the way. AvX, release Hugo immediately." Another explosion has us all ducking down, and I curl farther around Luna.

"Let's get the frack out of here, the whole place is unstable."

"Where is your shuttle?"

"Not far, let's go."

DaR yells, "Retreat, we got who we came for."

I start forward, only to stop when Hugo grabs my arm. "I'm not coming with you, there is supposed to be a shipment coming in today and if my resources are correct, these organics are all intact. I can't leave them here to die." I look around until I see a communicator hanging on EvO's side.

"EvO, do you have an extra communicator on you?"

"Always."

"Give it to Hugo, so that I can stay in contact with him here on the surface. Hugo, I will send a crew down to see what we can salvage from this sector. Thank you for all you have done for both of us… I will stay in contact."

"Thank you, Tordan…for looking past the male I once was and taking care of Luna; she has been through enough."

Luna trembles in my arms and I don't waste another minute. "DaR, get us out of here. Call SAGE, she is going to need Kira's med chamber."

"Absolutely not, you know no one is allowed to use that, it is to be available at all times in case of an emergency."

"DaR, this is not the time to test our friendship, because no matter the love I hold for you, the female I hold in my arms means more. I will destroy you to save her." DaR's eyes flash red, but he knows I'm serious.

"Stop it both of you. Father, sometimes I swear you can be so selfish. Tordan, there is another chamber on the Explorer. I will have it retrieved and on Falcor before we land."

"Thank you XuL."

DaR starts to say something, but I shake my head…we can talk later. I follow XuL as we race through the streets, our feet pounding the surface as I run full force toward the shuttles. We dart up the ramp and XuL heads straight to the captain's seat. I hear it closing and DaR cussing as he stomps his way up the hall.

"Impatient fracks, you about closed that damn ramp on my head."

I sit down, curling Luna's still limp form up on my lap. I lay my head down on top of hers, her pulse is weak, her body is bruised, and broken all over. "Come on little one, don't give up now, you have come so far." My heart breaks the more I look her over, what kind of male allows this to happen?

"Stop it Tordan, I can see it in your eyes...you need to stop thinking about her injuries and be thankful you got her out of there. You can brief me on what happened after we get her stable."

I know we were only in the air for a few moments, but it seems like a lifetime.

"Tordan, the medical crew will be awaiting our arrival and the Explorer just docked. Falcor is having the chamber moved to a private room as we speak. SAGE has linked the two chambers together so that she can monitor the female from planetside."

"Luna, her name is Luna." I'm standing at the ramp before we are even fully docked. I run down it toward the two healing bots waiting at the bottom. "General, please lay the female on the floater and we will proceed to the medical chamber."

I start to lower her down only to see her looking up at me. "We made it honey, we're safe...relax now, we're going to get you all fixed up."

In my mind, I hear her faintly... *"Don't leave mmeeee."*

Before I can answer her, the monitors on the bed light up red. "Sorry, General, we need to take it from here, we are losing her."

I hear someone cry out in anguish and a set of strong arms grab me. I fight against them until suddenly I'm picked up off the ground. I struggle to get free. I see the worry on my friend's faces, DaR and XuL look at me with nothing but concern on their faces and it takes me a moment to realize that sound is coming from me.

The moment I stop struggling against whoever is holding me. SoL's massive frame hovers, one of his large hands still holding onto my shoulder. "Sorry about having to manhandle you Tordan, but they needed to get her stabilized and you were in the way. If it makes you feel any better, Father couldn't hold onto you."

The sound of little feet and a squeal coming our way has me turning from all of them. A little green body flies toward me and I catch her midair. Small hands grab a hold of my face, tears flowing down her cheeks. "Unka Tordy you opay? I was so worried...look, you shiny all over." Keida's tiny arms grasp me tightly around the neck and I fall to my knees, overwhelmed. My own tears flow freely as I rock this precious child in my arms. Right now, she is the only thing grounding me as my thoughts and emotions are all over the place.

I have no idea how long I remain that way, but the sound of SAGE's voice has me standing back up with Keida still in my arms. XuL reaches for her, and I have to make myself let her go. She kisses me on the cheek and then wiggles for XuL to let her go. I watch her run off towards our private chambers. SAGE says my name twice I believe before I acknowledge her.

"General Tordan, can you come to the med center?"

"On my way."

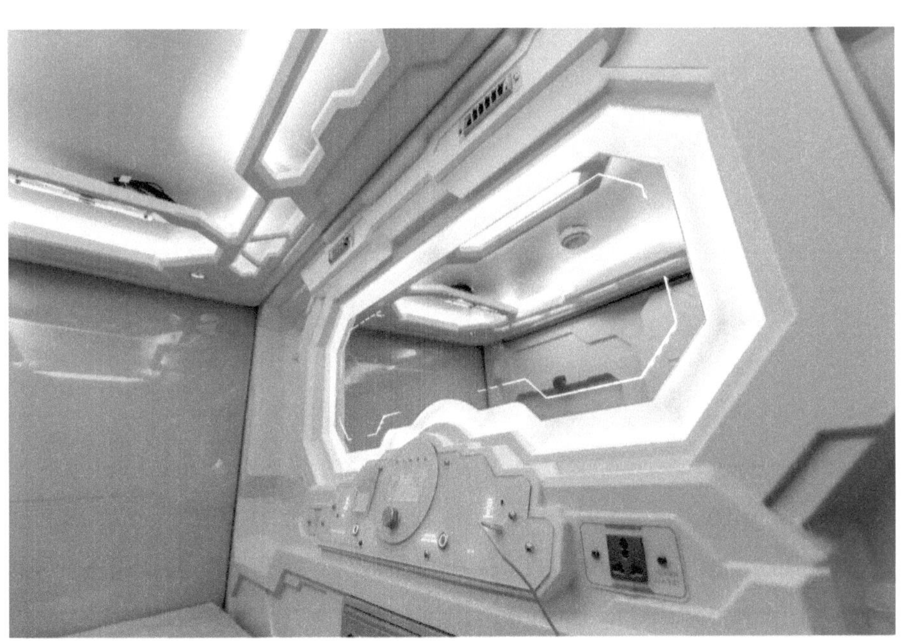

CHAPTER 22

TORDAN

I walk into the med chamber only to see what seems like a million tubes attached to Luna. I glance up at the screen above her body dreading what it was going to see, relieved that at least she is stabilized at this time.

"General, we need to discuss the female's health before we go forward."

"Her name is Luna."

"We have managed to stabilize Luna temporarily, but in the state her body is now, she will not last much longer if we don't act rapidly. Her bones can be mended, and we can provide her with some much-needed vitamins and nutrition to bring her body back to a healthy status. But, unfortunately, this treatment alone still won't save her. The metal that has been installed in her body is poisoning her blood. I believe she was healthy when they were initially connected, and she probably remained that way for some time. Until her liver started failing, she would not have shown any signs of deterioration. Unfortunately, once her system was contaminated with the poison of the metal it could no longer cleanse and filter it from her system. The bad nutrients and un-sterile environment she was in only accelerated her demise."

"What are you saying, we can fix her only for her to still die?"

"No, General, there is one other option, but I will need Tyberius and a plastic recreation specialist to complete the process. Because of the extent of these procedures, she will be in stasis for quite some time. The good news is the main med chamber can reverse the majority of her enhancements and her injuries.

"My initial scan shows that she has been inserted with a permanent feeding tube, that is something we will remove immediately. Her stomach is fine, she only needed the tube because her jaw and tongue were missing."

"Another good thing… the majority of her tongue is still there so it can be regrown. Her voice box is still mostly intact so we can restore a former version of her voice. Also, the skin on her cheeks can be grown to lengthen so that it will be connected seamlessly to her neck. Her jaw, I believe I can recreate and regenerate by taking a bone sample from the roof of her mouth. I would need the surgeon to recreate her mouth and lips, but I believe the success of this would be a huge improvement in her quality of life. Unfortunately, all that's left of her hand is metal. There is no flesh remaining I can build from, and the nerves are damaged where it wasn't connected properly. So, all we can do is install a prosthetic or a Cybernetic hand in its place. I believe Tyberius can help me with that, as the med chamber can't regrow anything that is completely missing."

"Can you smooth out the places that were ripped from her body? I don't care about them, but I could tell they made her extremely insecure."

"I believe so, yes…I can program the chamber to heal the majority of her scars also. Now all of this comes with its risk, but I do believe these procedures will provide the highest survival rate for her. If we leave her as she is now, she won't make it another lunar rotation."

"SAGE, what about her memories? They had a blocker inserted to make her more manageable."

"You have two choices, leave it in… and she will only know her years of captivity up to the present. Take it out… and hope that her mind is strong enough to handle everything at once because that's what it's going to be like for her. The only positive thing is she will have others to talk to that have been through similar experiences."

I stand here, how do you make a decision for someone else like this? She might hate me, or even mourn for a mate she already had on earth. My mind races with all the what IF's…

"Do everything you can for her SAGE, either way… at least she will live."

"Confirmed General, she will be moved and inserted into the med chamber momentarily. In the meantime, we need to get you looked over and see what's going on with your communicator. Falcor won't come right out and say it, but I believe he has missed your conversations and I know Commander DaR has been extremely worried."

"I'm fine."

DaR opens the door to the med chamber. "Get your ass on the bed Tordan, we can discuss what all happened down there while you are getting looked at. I didn't realize how empty my head was until I no longer had your cranky ass in it."

"Yeah, I missed you too, DaR." I climb up on the bed and practically fall back a huge sigh leaving my throat. "Frack, there for a moment I didn't think we were going to make it, especially when I couldn't get a hold of you… I had no idea how you were going to find me. As bad as I hate to say this, I should have listened and taken the backup you had suggested."

"I'm going to write this down. Tordan said I was right… All joking aside, at least you knew I was looking. I apologize that it took us so long, things have been tense since you left. I believe we have taken for granted how smoothly you run things around here. How is the female?"

"SAGE provided me with a positive outcome, but only time will tell. I have become attached rather quickly. Now that we are here, I worry…well, that she will want something more than I can provide."

"Let me warn you, now that you have found her, your life will never be the same. There are still darknesses that I lay there in bed simply holding Kira, wondering how I ever survived without her by my side. What makes me a terrible male is that I thank the Lord of Light for her losses because they granted me everything. Even though I'm truly ashamed of those feelings, I can't make them stop. I owe you an apology about the med chamber we have at the dwelling, but I can't stop my reactions when they come to Kira's safety. Her well-being is all that truly matters to me, and I know that makes me a selfish fracking male, but I can't help it. I would love to tell you that I would have granted you the use of it if XuL hadn't stepped in, but I'm simply glad that choice was taken from me."

The healing bots that come in to maneuver Luna to the med chamber interrupt our conversation. They are followed by one of the main healers on board. He comes in to program the machine. Once the screens turn green, he walks over to me.

"General, I'm pleased to hear you are back among us. Looking at you, I don't believe the Commander will allow you to head out alone in the future. Now, do you know how to retract this covering on your body?"

"Not a clue."

"Commander, do you have any ideas?"

"I believe once his body realizes he is no longer in danger, it will regress on its own. Something similar happened to Kira a while back."

He no longer says that then a chill racks my now naked body. DaR throws a nearby blanket over my lap. "Cover that thing up… But, Frack, Tordan you're beat all to hell."

"Yeah, and now I'm feeling it." The next thing I see is DaR's face fading.

CHAPTER 23

TORDAN

The sound of DaR's voice in my head awakens me. "Tordan, can you hear me?"

"Unfortunately, do you know that you just awoke me from one of the best sleeps of my entire existence?"

"Get your lazy ass up, Keida has been pacing at your door. She refuses to go play until she sees you again."

"Give me a second to get dressed DaR, and oh, by the way… it's good to have your growly, gruff voice back in my head. SAGE, update me on Luna… and how long have I been out?"

"Only two risings, General, your wounds are healed, and you should be good as new. Luna is doing well, and everything is right on schedule."

"Falcor, open the outer door for Keida."

"Confirmed, it's nice to have you back in operations, sir."

"Wow, Falcor, for a second there I almost thought you missed me. I believe that's the most words I have ever heard from you at once."

Before Falcor can respond, little arms grab my legs, hugging them tightly. I reach down, picking her up. "Is this a new dress? You look beautiful this rising."

"Thank you, Mamaw made it for me, but I won't be wearing them much longer. Papaw is having a big girl like me, and Daddy named Zura to come teach me how to fight. Ever since the dark man was here, Papaw decided all us girls will learn to defend ourselves, even the big girls like Mommy and Mamaw have to do it."

"The dark man."

"Yea, the one that turns all invisible, like the wind."

"He was here on Falcor?"

"Yea, Danny made him go away. Mom said Danny was a badass…but I got in trouble when I said it." She shrugs. "Then Unka SoL started yelling and I had to put my hands over my ears. His voice is too big when he gets all growly. Did you know, I missed you really bad. One night I was sad because I had a bad dream about you, and I didn't want to go back to sleep. So, Falcor read me my bedtime stories until you got back."

"Did he now?"

"Yea, him just shy around the grownups…him plays with me and Dan all the time. He was very upset the dark man got past his sensors and almost got me and Mamaw."

"I'm pretty upset about that, too."

"Will I have someone new to play with soon? I saw you bring in another girl. Is she big like Mommy and Mamaw?"

"She is, but right now she is with the doctor. I hope she will be out soon, and I'm sure she will love you as much as I do."

"Well, I better go. I have a date."

"And here I thought you got all dressed up for me? Who is the lucky male?"

"I'm meeting Danny in the conservatory. We are going to have a picnic"

"Well, go on and have a good time, I'm going to go check on my own girl." She kisses me on the cheek, and I lower her back down to the floor, watching as she skips from the room.

"Falcor, I believe the youngling has given up one of your secrets. I appreciate you leaving the security of your programming to comfort her."

"I reacted out of character, Sir, but the youngling was having visions. She sees things she shouldn't for one so young. After the first darkness on board, I sprayed a light sedative in her and the boy's room, just enough for her to go into a deep sleep and not a dream sleep."

"I want you to do something completely against your programming and I want this conversation and all procedures marked from your records. The next darkness when you know both the younglings are once again sleeping deeply, I want you to install an untraceable tracking chip into each of them. No one is to know of this but us…is that understood?"

"Approved and confirmed. I will notify you when this has been completed."

"One more thing, Falcor. How did SiN gain access to this ship?"

"I'm ashamed to say, but at the exact time he boarded. SCOUT had informed us that he had a possible lock on your location, and I turned all sensors towards Targres Four, trying to contact you. I know that was a rash and unauthorized action. I gave the report of my actions to SoL, and I await further discipline for my actions."

"In other words, you were looking for me."

"Affirmative."

"I can't help but smile, unfeeling bastard my ass."

"The Commander is awaiting your presence in the control room. They are discussing the capture of SiN. He says these acts of violence on the family will no longer be tolerated."

"On my way."

CHAPTER 24

LUNA

The sound of someone pecking on a glass wakes me up. I open my eyes, blinking them a few times only to see a streak of green and pink flash across what looks like a screen in front of me. Then I hear what sounds like air brakes on a dump truck and the screen slides down and away. The surface I'm lying on opens up wider, almost like I was cocooned. I have never seen this place before, there are no arms hanging from the ceilings, or any instruments anywhere, just some sort of soft music playing.

"SAGE, she is awake, I'll go get Unka Tordy."

The sound of a child's voice has me jerking straight up, only to catch a door closing out of the corner of my eye.

"Sorry about that, she gets rather excited…easily. Please don't be alarmed, you are safe and Tordan will be here within moments. He just stepped out when the chamber notified me it was opening. Here is a nightgown. I have learned from experience most females are calmer when clothed."

My heart is beating out of my chest. *Where am I?* I look around to see if there is anyone else in the room, but just like AMI… the voice seems to be everywhere. I grab the gown and barely have it down over my hips when the door opens up again and a little girl with a pale green face jumps up on the side of what I think is a bed.

"Hi, my name is Keida, wow you are so pretty now…SAGE rocks at this build-a-girl thing she does… When you first got here, Unka Tordy was really sad, and I had to give him one of those hugs… You know the ones that make all the pain go away. He hasn't left your side and you have been in here a long time."

She grabs my hand. "Do you like to play? I really hope so! Mamaw just made me a new baby to play with, maybe I can show you later… She says I'm spoilt."

I reach up slowly with my other hand, running my fingers through her long dark hair, it has beautiful pink and white stripes throughout it. Her little green ears are pointed, but it's her mesmerizing pink eyes I can't seem to stop staring at. The child is absolutely beautiful.

"Who are you?" *Did I just say that out loud? Or was it in my head?*

The little girl tilts her head, she suddenly looks puzzled. "I think Mommy or Mamaw would be better at answering all that, but I'm glad you're awake. I have so much stuff to show you."

I jerk when a three-foot-high image pops up on the bottom of the bed. "Sorry, no matter how many times I do that, I still seem to startle everyone. I'm SAGE, by the way. I hope that we can become great friends, and this little green bundle of energy is Keida. Her sidekick is a human male named Danny, but I'm not sure exactly where he is at the moment.

"Keida, sweetheart, why don't you go tell Kira and Brit that she is awake and maybe have them prepare a nice lunch for everyone? Let's give Luna a moment to herself."

The little girl jumps off the bed and I watch her rush out of the room. I take a minute to look around; the hologram doesn't say anything else; she simply stands at the foot of the bed. I don't know what I'm feeling, my mind is sorta numb. I feel…different.

TORDAN AND TYBERIUS

I stand on the other side of the viewing wall, watching Keida practically bouncing up and down on the foot of Luna's bed. We all talked about it and decided Keida was the best option for when she awakened. The child is so naturally bubbly that everyone immediately feels relaxed around her.

I hear Tyberius open the door, then he walks up behind me. "I heard she had awakened and thought I should come check on her progress. One good thing... at least she didn't wake up screaming, we will count that as a blessing. I will say, I'm impressed with the final results. There were a few times I was worried her body wasn't going to accept the medical nanites I used to attach her hand, but that med chamber being a scientific miracle worker helped her right along with the process. I have never seen it literally piece someone back together the way it did her. She should be in optimal health now and at the prime of her human life."

"Ty, I never asked, but now that I have been through all of this, how did you grow my arm? ENAC was doing everything he could to recreate it. He said he had your records, but nothing he was doing was working. You saw firsthand how those half-assed cybernetics were attached to Luna."

"Ahh, I knew one day your curiosity would get the better of you. Honestly, I'm shocked it has taken you so long to ask me. Tordan, when I pulled you out of that building, you were practically torn in half. I had no idea if there was any way possible to save you, your injuries …were so severe. We…I… didn't have the knowledge of how to fix you. Not only had you lost an arm, but your ribs and lung were destroyed…half your face was smashed. I remember looking over at DaR as he was standing over you in the hospital, his grief was so strong that his Symbots were walking all over him, trying to give him some sort of comfort.

"I was fumbling around, struggling to hook you up to a life support chamber, trying my best to get you stabilized. I wasn't a healer, and I definitely wasn't authorized to do those types of procedures, but there were so many fatalities and injuries from the explosion. I was the only hope you had. Anyway, I saw one of DaR's Symbots reach out and touch a cut you had on your leg, and it healed within moments. I had seen them do this to him thousands of times, but it never occurred to me that they…could be transferred to another.

"DaR's Symbots are a part of him and have been with him since his birth, a gift from his mother's side. I never saw them as anything other than protection specifically linked to his personal essence. See, DaR's Symbots are alive, they pick and choose who they will protect. Even on his mother's home planet, very few are gifted with them.

"So, I took a chance, and I simply asked them if they would help me save your life. I wasn't expecting an answer or even any type of movement. DaR has a way of communicating with them, but I didn't know if they understood any of the others around them.

"DaR reached down and put his hand over your chest; he was simply heartbroken that he was going to lose his best friend. You were not just a male he played with but a male who had become the brother he never had.

"I believe it was his grief that made them help you. A small section released from his arm and crawled upon your skin. I stood back in complete amazement as they took over. You see, the truth is, I didn't make your arm or do any of the reconstructive surgery. They did, and they have grown with you from that moment on. I don't know why they took on the look of cybernetics or why they have reacted differently on you than they do DaR. But the one thing I was able to do was to hide what had been done…it made a way for me to doctor up the records and the procedure."

"I can't believe DaR knew this all this time and never told me."

"I swore him to secrecy…if something like that got out…well, I don't have to tell you the consequences.

"No one questioned or even asked me much about it, they were simply glad we found a way to save you. Since then, your blood is like DaR's, it's rich with their natural medical compounds. I figured we had nothing to lose with Luna, so I simply pulled some of it from you and inserted it into her, hoping that the Symbots would help with the attachment, and they did.

"Not only did this make her hand look and work the same as her natural one, but the medical nanites will strengthen her internally. She will have a longer life span, more than likely matching your own since they come from you. Now we simply have to wait and see how her mind deals with the past and present.

"Unfortunately, She will have to learn to speak and eat again. I know SAGE did her best with recreating her facial reconstruction, but honestly, she may look nothing like she remembers. You will have to be patient with her, everything she has gone through…well, it seems more intense than the others.

"On a personal note…I also noticed that your fangs have not retracted. I will warn you it's the smell of her blood that your body is reacting to. You are a true-born Darverions, the same as all the elders who crashed along with me on Earth. There is not a big enough warning I can give you… but you can never give into the temptation of her blood.

"First of all, you would go into a bloodlust, an absolute frenzy that you could not control. Not only would you drain her dry, tearing her to pieces in the process. You would be a threat to every human female here. Because I can guarantee you no matter how strong you think you are. The thirst will consume you... I was sure that I would be stronger than the thirst, there was no way I could become the monster the others did, but I failed... and it controlled me, for centuries. I destroyed lives, and in the end, it almost destroyed me.

"Second, the Blood Beet would no longer be enough to sustain your system, you would have to add human blood to your diet to survive. Our human females all donate to 'the keep the vampires alive club,' that's what Brit has named it, but I don't know if they could provide for all of us. I only warn you of this, because no one here but me truly understands how tempting she is for you. I have had centuries to conquer my thirst and the temptation. It will take you some time to adjust, and I mean even if she gets a paper cut on her finger, don't taste it."

"I'm glad you made me aware that it was her blood calling out to me. I wonder why none of the other females affected me so?"

"We all do have our favorite flavors, and apparently, she is yours. She is quite lovely. I'm so used to all of our females having such long hair that her short curls make her look younger than she truly is."

"I'm Orbital rotations older than her, Ty, I should find a way to back out of her life and let one of the younger males woo her."

"We are our worst enemies, Tordan, we always think how much better others would be without us. What we tend to not see is how much the other may need you. She trusts you then and she will now. If you walk away, you will lose your only reason for breathing. I don't believe the Lord of Light has us walking on any path he didn't originally want us on. Be what she needs, if, in the end, she craves something else you both will know.

"You have to remember you are not the only male here who has said those exact words. We are all much older than our females. I alone have centuries on my Victoria, and it's never been an issue…if anything they will make you feel younger. I also believe it's made me a better male to her as I was no longer plagued by stupidity and bad decisions of youth.

"She is here, and you are both safe, you have come to care for this female. I know no other who deserves the happiness you will only come to enjoy in her arms. Don't make problems in your own head."

We both stand there watching her look around the room, she appears so small sitting upon the med chamber's mainframe. I struggle with what to do, what if I am nothing to her but a forced bad memory? What if the emotional encounter we had in that room meant more to me than it did her? What if I am only a reminder of the horrors she has gone through?

Then it hits me… "Ty, was she…is she with child?"

"I saw no evidence of any sort of pregnancy, as a matter of fact, she still had extensive scarring inside her reproductive organs. Her body was in such a frail state, I don't believe her system would have accepted the embryo, but that's not the case now. She is a very healthy and fertile female, so if you don't want a little Tordan running around you may want to watch what you are doing until you both decide you want more."

I'm relieved and sad all at the same time.

CHAPTER 25

LUNA

"Luna, I have locked the door to give you a moment to yourself. I know Tordan is probably pacing back and forth outside the door as we speak, but I feel like you may want a moment to absorb the sudden changes in your environment and yourself. Can you tell me what you remember last? We upgraded your personal communicator so I can hear you if you are not comfortable trying to speak."

"Tordan… he was trying to get us out of the compound. It's all in pieces."

"I will let him explain what happened after your escape, but right now let's talk about you. Are you hurting anywhere?"

I shake my head no. Then it dawns on me, that nothing hurts. I look up at the hologram.

"Do you think you have the strength to take a couple of steps on your own? I believe you need to see something."

I slide off the side of the bed, expecting a cold floor under my feet, but the floor is soft and warm instead. The room itself is plain but comfortable, and for some reason, that feels odd to me. It's almost like I have gotten used to being cold and uncomfortable. I stand here for a second looking around, then I take a few unstable steps away from the bed.

The holo disappears off the bed only to show back up on the floor in front of me. "I'm going to open a viewing wall for you," she says hesitantly to me.

A huge mirror appears right out of the air in front of...me. I stand here not sure what or who is in the image. The girl standing there looks familiar, but I don't know who it is.

"Who is that?"

"You!"

I'm not sure of the what or the who that I can hear, but someone is screaming. The agonizing sound tugs at my heart. Whoever it is, their whole world has come crashing down around them. Suddenly, I start to see dark spots in front of my eyes, the walls are closing in, and I sway on my feet.

I watch through a stranger's eyes as everything comes back at once. Wait... I was taken. My father, running...the horror in his eyes. My mom, family, friends, all my hopes, and dreams were destroyed. Aliens...the never-ending pain, then it was like I started living a whole other existence, simply putting one foot in front of the other for… years. I believe I may have even died once… They took my very identity and I let them until…Tordan. Where is Tordan? How did I get here…where is here? Who are these people?"

I feel my legs buckle under me, but before I can hit the floor, strong arms grab me. I'm shaking all over.

"Hey, little one, I got you! Take a few deep breaths for me, you are safe. "

I cry out, grabbing onto the first familiar thing my mind can recognize, and practically crawl up his body. Tordan sits down on the floor with me curled up in his lap rocking me back and forth rubbing my back gently. I tuck my head under his chin trying my best to crawl into his skin. I have no idea how long we sat that way. He didn't say a word, he simply sat there holding me.

I open my eyes when my mind seems to calm down, only to see a hand laying against his chest. I pull my other arm out from around him and slowly sit up. I hold both hands up… Then I look up at Tordan; I know my face is full of questions.

He lifts me effortlessly, turning me back towards the mirror. If I didn't know I was in his lap. I would think he was holding someone else.

"I can tell by the look on your face that you're confused. So, I will try to explain what I can… I'm not sure where to start, honestly. I'm scared that no matter what I say you will hate me for it, but here goes nothing… I made a decision that I had no right to do when it comes to you or any other… You see, you were moments from death, the metal that ENAC and AMI had inserted into your body was…did poison you. By the time the healer discovered where the poison was coming from… there were only minutes to decide on whether I could let you go…

"I refused to lose you, I would rather you hate me and still be breathing than the thought of never holding you again. I felt then… and I still do, at least. Worst case scenario, one rising you could possibly forgive me for my selfishness. I had the means and the equipment to save your life, and selfishly I made that decision for you. I couldn't let you go."

I reach up, touching the face in the mirror, then look back at my hands again; they look the same. I pull the nightgown away from the inside of my legs and there are no hunks missing from my skin, but the person in the mirror is not me.

"Did you somehow put my mind in another's body?"

"Nope, this is all you…or as close as we could get anyway. Your body was repaired and I had all traces of the horrors you had experienced erased from your skin. I know I can't take the memories away, but I was hoping to take away the physical pain at least. SAGE recreated the lower half of your face. Luna, I can tell by the way you are looking at your reflection, that it's not as you remember… Is your name even Luna?"

"Yes, Luna Inez Porter. Is your real name Tordan?"

"I had no reason to lie to you about my name, as ENAC already knew who I was, but formally, I am General Tordan Zyair, second in command of the starship Falcor and protector of Darverius. That is where you are now, safely… on Falcor with my family and friends. Tell me what you see in the mirror, let's see if you can talk."

I don't know how to do what he is asking me. I lean forward a little, bringing my face right up to the wall. I run my hand down my cheeks as I turn my new face one way then another. My skin is flawless, and the long scar that had run from the top of my forehead all the way down my cheek is gone. It takes me a couple of times, but I'm able to wiggle my chin back and forth.

I slowly open my mouth expecting gums, only to see beautiful, straight white teeth instead. Tears come to my eyes again. I always wanted straight teeth as a kid, but we couldn't afford braces. The moment that memory hits me the pain becomes fresh all over again. I turn from the mirror, straddling Tordan's lap. I tuck my hands in between us and crawl in as close as I can.

It's too much, I don't know how to sort through this mess that's now in my head. He picks us up off the ground and I hear him tell the hologram something and a door opens. It's like I'm watching it all happen to someone else. I don't feel attached to my own skin.

There are voices all around and I put my hands over my ears as tears flow down my cheeks. I wrap my legs around his waist, clinging to him for dear life. Everything is too noisy. When an odd hand touches my back I flinch and pull away. I just want it all to stop, I don't want to remember…it's all too new. I feel like it's all happening all over again.

Suddenly, it's quiet, and I let myself take a breath. Tordan doesn't say anything, he just walks around, holding me in his arms. I honestly feel like a small child he is packing around trying to keep her from throwing a temper tantrum and I don't care. His strong arms are the only place I feel safe…and then I remember them forcing me onto him…sexually.

LUNA

"To.r..an. I s.ry." It's all I can force out. My throat feels raw and talking seems so foreign to me. I haven't spoken or smiled, even taken a bite of food, in so long. I don't really remember how.

"Don't force it, Luna. I didn't have your communicator removed. Once again, because I'm a selfish bastard and I wanted to be able to talk to you no matter where you were, but also because I knew it would take you a little bit to adjust. So, you can talk to me like you have always done. Why are you sorry?"

"I'm clinging to you like you're my own personal safety line. You were forced to…to have sex with me." I try to squirm out of his arms only for him to pull me tighter.

"I'm not putting you down, so quit squirming and go ahead and finish that thought, then I'll tell you what I think of it."

"I don't want you to feel like you have to take care of me… well, more than you already have. I know firsthand the horrors of being forced and the fact that you have taken care of me…even though you may hate me, just shows what a good man you are. I don't know if the situation had been reversed if I would have made the same decisions you have. I'm so sorry they hurt you. I'm sorry you got trapped trying to save me. I'm sorry I didn't help you escape." I put my arms around his neck and simply cry. *"I'm a damn mess and I have no idea how to make it all better."*

"My poor, sweet girl, you have not heard a word I have said. First of all, have you really looked at me? I'm a big male, and if I had not wanted to have sex with you no amount of drugs or force could have made me. Yes, I gave in because I didn't want you punished, but mating you was no hardship on my end. Now would I have loved for you to recognize from the very beginning that I was the good guy and that I was willing to do anything to get you out of there? Absolutely, but life never takes the easy route. But that's ok because we are here together now.

"You are not beholden to me or any other. You now have choices in your life, like where you want to go, where you want to live, and who you want to be with. Your situation may seem dire right now, as it's all so new to you, but I give you my word. I will find a way to make you happy. I want to see those bright blue eyes of yours light up with mischief and a huge smile on your face Every rising.

"Realistically, there will still be quite a bit of things you won't be happy hearing. Not including the ongoing pain of your memories and the stuff you have experienced. But, hopefully, it will all get easier in time, because I plan on giving you plenty of good memories to replace the bad with.

"I know I keep saying this, but I don't own you. You are in charge of your future even if you find another male more worthy of you. Don't get me wrong, it would destroy me to let you go, but your happiness is all that matters. You are not a prisoner here and you will soon learn, how easily you females get by with everything. I value your independence and I pray to the Lord of Light that you see me as more than someone you were forced upon, but as a male who wants you in whatever form you come in.

"Luna, we were thrown into a very bad situation together and I hope that with that experience, if nothing else comes of it, you know I'm here for you. We don't know each other well and I understand that, but I'm not going anywhere. We have been blessed with another chance at happiness and I refuse to let the past or others take that gift from us.

"I don't want you to feel like you are obligated to have to stay here with me either. If you want a room of your own I completely under-stand. I anticipated that you might want some personal space while you are healing. So, I had a suite prepared for you off of mine, but if you would allow it, I would rather hold you this darkness.

"I feel like you have just been given back to me. I watched or monitored that med chamber nonstop … one moment it would be green, and I would breathe a little easier knowing you were being healed. Then alarms would go off and it would turn red, and the fear of losing you would practically take me to my knees. So right now, I'm not sure who is comforting whom."

I just hug him tighter. I don't know if I'm strong enough to do anything but hold on at this point, and I don't want to make any decisions. After a few minutes, I feel him lean down as he pulls my legs away from his waist, and he lays us down on a huge, soft surface. A soft blanket is draped over us moments later and just the feeling of being safe in his arms has me crying all over again. At some point, I must have cried myself to sleep because the bed moving has me opening my eyes and I instantly reach out for him.

"Go back to sleep, little one, I have a few things I have to do this rising, but I won't be long." He kisses me on the forehead then stands above the bed looking down at me. I can see he is struggling with leaving me.

"Luna, call out if you need me, and I'll come right away. The personal refreshing room, or bathroom as you females call it, is through that doorway. If you need something you can't find in there, all you have to do is ask SAGE or Falcor. They are always here with us, similar but less invasive than AMI. Do you understand?"

I shake my head yes, and pull the blanket around me tighter, enjoying the softness of it against my skin. I watch him walk out of the room, then I just lay there looking around. I finally raise up, leaning back against the wall. The room is actually very nice,

I'm even kind of shocked to see a few random trinkets here and there.

Its main colors are burgundy and gray. Oddly, enough it's the pillows laying on the large couches that make the place seem homier. Tordan is full of surprises because decorating wasn't something I would have put on his resume. I lay here, simply enjoying the silence picking apart the things that have happened to me in these past years one small piece at a time. Refusing to focus on any one thing for very long, as I have always hated crying, and I feel like that's all I have been doing since I opened my eyes.

I hate to leave the comfort and security of this bed, but the urge to pee won't go away so I force myself to get up.

"Good rising, Mistress Luna, would you enjoy a bath this morning?"

"I can have an honest-to-goodness bath? Like with water and everything?"

"You sure can, I'll get it prepared for you. It's nice to see you in better spirits this rising."

CHAPTER 27

LUNA

I walk into the bathroom hesitantly, only to be surprised at how familiar it all is. I stand in the middle of it looking around, beyond happy to see a normal commode and a real bathtub in front of me. I run my fingers underneath the water coming out of a waterfall-type fixture in the wall and feel myself smile for the first time.

"The water is ready whenever you are Luna, relax and enjoy a few moments to yourself."

"SAGE... Right?"

"Yes Mistress, all you need to do is to call out and I'm available anytime."

I discard the gown I have on and step into the hot water. My skin immediately turns pink as I sink down into the water clear up to my neck. I don't think I have felt anything this good in…well I have no idea actually, and if this is a dream or just an old memory, that's fine too. I'm simply going to go with it.

I have no idea how long I have laid here, merely basting in the warmth that seems to have finally sunk into my very bones, but the temptation of using soap is calling my name. Taking each one of the bottles off the ledge, I smell them one at a time, inhaling one of them longer than the others when I recognize it smells just like Tordan.

I try to imagine his large frame in this tub surrounded by bubbles and an actual partial laugh leaves my smiling lips. I wash my skin over and over until it's raw in places. Refusing to focus on any one particular spot for long, or the bad memories come back in full force. Finally, when I feel wilted all over, I let the water out and stand up, looking for something to dry off with.

I gasp when a cabinet drawer opens out of nowhere and a towel raises out of it. I dry off then wrap it around me tightly, only to realize I have nothing to put on.

"SAGE is there anything of Tordan's I could possibly wear? I don't feel comfortable walking around in just this."

"I have something even better. I have CIP. He is a Custom Imprint Printer and a master in the design of clothing. I will generate you a few items momentarily, and then we can look at a few options that you will be comfortable in until we can get you a wardrobe made."

I walk over to the huge mirror that takes up the whole wall, hesitating a second before forcing myself to drop the towel. I stand there naked, allowing myself the time to become comfortable with this new me. The more my eyes run over my features the more familiar they seem. Yes, I have changed, and things are not exact, but that's me in the mirror.

I have always been on the small side, mostly because of how physical it was to keep the farm up, and then…well, I'm not going to think about the rest. Instead, I decide to focus on the things that made me who I am. Like the fact that Dad didn't raise a quitter. I can hear his words in my head and if I think about it hard enough, I can still smell Mom baking cookies and her perfume. I concentrate on those memories, willing their happiness to be my foremost thoughts.

I close my eyes, giving myself a second to reflect. Then I start to evaluate the differences in my new appearance. There are no huge chunks of skin missing from my legs or hips now. My skin is smooth, and my muscles are more prominent than ever. My stomach and waistline are still slightly sunken in, but I don't look starved, just small. I have to make myself look at my right breast, expecting to see most of it missing, but there isn't a mark on it. My face…is odd though.

The hologram appears floating in the mirror, looking back at me. "I'm glad to read that your vital signs are not elevated. I was truly worried that my measurements and calculations had been completely wrong when it came to your appearance, but from my point of view, you are quite beautiful. It amazes me the differences in the features and builds of all human females. Would you like me to tell you a little about the process?

"I have always felt like the more information a person or machine has, the better they deal with things in the future. The other females seemed to adapt easier the more they knew about their circumstances, than when they didn't."

"There are others here like me?"

"Yes and no…you will meet them all soon, and then they can tell you their stories themselves.

"Now back to you. I'm going to start with your face. I searched for records of you from ANDI's archives and couldn't find anything that had a picture of you from the front. So, I took measurements from the other females and compared them to yours, and then recreated your chin and jawline. If genetics were perfect, this is what you would have always looked like, but of course, we know there is no such thing as flawless when it comes to individual creation.

"I had to bring in a Reconstructive Reparative Healer to help with recreating your mouth, teeth, and lips. These reconstructions being new, will be a little harder to use at first because the muscles have to be exercised. The more you move your mouth, such as eating or even trying to talk as you wake your voice box back up, the more natural it will feel and before long you will be as you once were.

"Now, even though your fleshly body went through unholy horrors, the strengths you obtained in your previous life are what kept you alive. You were healthy when taken, all besides your reproductive organs, and because of that you were not hard to mend. Your muscle and skin tones are your own, simply healed from the inside out. The scarring your body sustained, I lasered away. You have enough to work through without having to be reminded every rising of the past. The only thing I couldn't give you back was your hand.

I hold my hand out, trying to figure out what she is talking about. *"I don't understand."*

"The med chamber cannot regrow anything that is truly missing. There has to be at least a small piece for it to attach to. Your hand was completely cybernetic, and a faulty one at that. Tyberius, the male who gave Tordan his cybernetic arm, helped to fuse the same type of material into your nervous system. Then I grafted the skin over the metal to make it look the same as your other one. The only thing is your fingernails won't grow on that hand."

That rough laugh leaves my throat again. *"Fingernails are the least of my worries. You said something about my reproductive organs?"*

"Yes, the med chamber was able to heal the scarring inside of your uterus, so in the future, you will be able to bear young."

"I had no idea...you know, before I was taken, that I couldn't have children."

"I don't want to bring up any bad emotions, but again I feel like knowledge is everything. So please forgive me for this ahead of time, but that's the reason you were rejected and torn apart by the Banham's. They sent the Korgons to earth to capture females of certain ages. If that female was considered faulty, she was separated from the others that could breed, and you know first-hand how that turns out. You were not the only one here put through such horrors, but like I mentioned before that is not my story to tell."

"You are right, it's not easy to hear but thank you for the truth…and for all you have done for me." A tear rolls down my cheek and I brush it away. *"I'm so lost…what do I do now? I have questions, but I'm terrified of the answers."*

"You need to take it one step at a time. How about we get you dressed and fed? Tordan is on his way back now and I can tell he has been stressed being away from you."

I nod my head yes…. SAGE disappears for a moment only to reappear on the other side of the room. The whole wall seems to disappear, only to open up into a huge closet. She waves me forward and I grab the towel I had dropped onto the floor, wrapping it back around myself.

I walk into the other room hesitantly, rows of different clothing and supplies line the place. Sage points to a small section hanging alone. "I promise this is only temporary, soon you will have so much we will have to have Falcor expand this area. I have provided you with a couple of options for now. The other females seem to enjoy these designs more than some of the others and because I'm so intimate with your measurements, they should fit you perfectly."

A drawer pulls out of the bottom, with several different kinds of panties laying in the bottom. I let the towel drop and pick up a neutral bikini pair. *"No bras?"*

"We have designed them to be part of the garment, makes the dress more comfortable."

I pull a pale green sundress off a hanger and then slip it over my head. A pair of matching sandals appear, and I slide them on my feet. Like she said it all fits perfectly, it's nice to finally feel like a human again.

I hear a knock on the door. "Luna, if you feel like it, would you like to take a walk with me?"

CHAPTER 28

LUNA

I look over at the mirror one last time, running my fingers through the damp, short curls on my head. Finally, I shrug when I realize nothing I do is going to make them lie down.

I walk forward once again, shocked to see the wall just disappear, *That is definitely going to take some time to get used to.* Tordan has his back to me at first only to turn when he hears my footsteps.

"Hi," I manage to squeak out.

He just stands there looking at me, I smooth my hands down the knee-length skirt, making sure I didn't have it stuck in my panties or something.

"Look at you! Luna, honey, you are a sight to behold. Beautiful!"

I smile and shake my head, no…even though I enjoy the words as I can tell he truly means it.

"I was going to take you for a walk around the ship, but now I think I'll just hide you away in my quarters forever and keep you for myself." He approaches me slowly sliding his hand against my cheek as he runs his thumb over my lower lip. "You ok?"

"I won't lie and say that I am, but what I will tell you is that I will be. I'm sure I'll fall apart on a regular basis, but I have not made it this far only to lay down and let those monsters steal the rest of my life, however long that is. If you say I'm safe, then I believe you. I trust you Tordan, and the number of people I have ever said those words to can be counted on one hand, please don't let me down. I'm struggling with every step forward. My mind is only one more disappointment from shattering."

"I'm honored and terrified, but if you're willing we will walk this path slowly forward together."

"I would like that."

"How about we start with food?"

"It's a date."

Tordan holds my hand as we make our way through a long hallway. We enter into what looks like a cafeteria and I'm shocked that as large as this is, we are the only ones here.

"Where is everyone?" And Lord it just hits me, I'm on an alien ship. *"Maybe, it would be better if we did return to your room. I don't want to flip out on you because we run into one of those yellow flesh eaters or blue beasts."*

"If you run into a Banham on this ship, then it's a ghost because DaR destroyed both them and the Korgons in this region…

including their slave trade. You will eventually meet other species, but any aboard Falcor has been picked personally either by DaR or myself. There isn't a male here that I would not think twice about allowing to protect you or the others.

"Right now, Falcor has part of the ship sectioned off because we have multiple females on board,…your safety is a top priority. And when it comes to Kira, DaR has always been slightly over-protective… With the addition of each of the females, he is only getting worse. I used to think he was being absurd, but now I completely understand.

"When you are ready, we will discuss the species that took you from your home, but not this rising. Come, let's think of better things like what would you like to try to eat. I know you have to be hungry as it's been two risings since you have awakened."

"To be honest, food has been an afterthought for so long that I really hadn't even noticed I was hungry. I know you don't have a Snickers bar or a Pepsi anywhere around here, so why don't you just pick me something? I haven't eaten anything solid in so long, I'm not sure if I will be able to remember how to swallow."

"Have a seat. I will see what I can find."

I sit down and almost jerk right back up when the seat starts to form around me. *Lord, is everything alienish?* I take a moment to actually look at Tordan. I don't know if I have ever met anyone who moves as fluidly as he does. His body is huge, but he glides along almost like he is floating above the floor, his large feet not making a sound. I miss the fact that he was always shirtless before, but the cut of his uniform still leaves little to the imagination. Even with his oddness, there is no denying he is quite handsome, or maybe his face has just become precious to me.

He has a couple of plates in his hands and starts to turn back to me, only to go back and get something else. That squeaky laugh leaves my throat again as he just keeps putting plates on the table. "Tor..n...cnt..et..all," I try to force the words out, but they are broken up.

"Don't force your voice, it will come back on its own before you know it. Yes, I know you can't eat all of this, but I have no idea what you might want. Try something soft first. See how your throat does with it before you try anything solid or spicy."

Simply picking up a fork to eat seems odd. I look over the plates, pulling a few closer to me. Then I poke at what looks like eggs only to end up smearing them on my face instead of hitting my mouth.

Tordan doesn't say a word, he simply takes the fork out of my hand and scoots me closer in between his legs. He wipes the bottom of my face off and I feel myself start to tear up. He wipes a single tear off my cheek, acting like he doesn't even see it, and this helps me get my emotions back under control.

Picking the food up between his fingers he moves it toward my mouth slowly. "Open your mouth, and just let me feed you. I'm going to give you small pieces until your jaws start working properly."

It takes me a few tries, but finally, I'm chewing slowly. I almost get choked on the first swallow, but each one gets easier. After a few pieces, he would trade out what I just ate for something else, making me practically relearn with every bite. Amongst feeding me, he would shove enough food in his mouth to feed me for a week. He catches me smiling after one extremely large mouthful and shrugs his shoulders. "Can't help it, I require lots of fuel to keep this frame going."

I push his hand back, finally not being able to take another bite, but it's nice to feel full for a change. My jaw seems a little sore, but I feel like I was finally getting the hang of it again.

"You ready for that walk?"

"Yep," I squeak again.

Tordan picks up the plates taking them to what looks like a garbage can disposing them inside and then comes back to me, grabbing my hand, pulling me forward.

"Wait, where is Hugo? I promised not to leave without him?"

"He is safe, and on a mission of his own. I can put you in contact with him later if you want."

I shake my head yes.

"Let me show you, my baby."

Falcor is a marvel of pure perfection and Tordan is the best tour guide ever. It doesn't help that I simply enjoy listening to him talk either. He explains everything I am seeing in great detail. So that

I can understand the workings of the ship and the things around me. The ship was designed with its residence in mind, from its soft colors to the pleasant smell coming out of the vents. He explains how different parts of the ship are sectioned off, from recreation to weapons.

He even takes the time to tell me about how Falcor became the main defense starship in this solar system. His enthusiasm just kept the questions coming from me, and I was content with him simply showing me the things he thought I would want to see until he told me that even though Falcor's primary home was orbiting Darverius. There had been times he had to be launched into space for an extended amount of time. So, the ship not only had personal quarters for every residence, but also a major medical center, and a whole floor dedicated to growing the food the personnel would need for extended trips. Falcor was completely self-sufficient.

"Can I see that floor? The one where you grow everything."

"Absolutely, it never dawned on me that you may be interested in seeing that any further."

"Tordan, I was raised on a farm, that's what we did. We raised crops for others to eat, I'm more comfortable with my hands in the dirt than anywhere." Tordan pulls me towards him as we get into what looks like a tube, then touches an invisible button that I didn't see quickly enough. I screech a little when it feels like we have been shot into the air by an invisible floor. His laughing makes me realize I have practically crawled up his large frame.

"I don't mind holding you at all, little one, just release those claws of yours out of my side and I will happily carry you from this point on."

I slide back down and straighten my dress up. He pulls me back, kissing my forehead and I feel my whole body relax. It's crazy how quickly I have come to care about him, but he is just so easy to be around.

When the wall does that complete disappearing thing, I walk forward in a daze.

CHAPTER 29

LUNA

I don't know what is more overwhelming, the smell of dirt, or the planet that looks like Saturn hovering through the clear dome overhead.

"Is that Saturn?"

"No that's Sybrus Two, it's one of the three moons that orbit Darverius and that's not the only difference from your solar system. We also have two suns."

I let go of Tordan's hand and walk forward. There are rows and rows of beds lifted above the floor. Of course, I don't recognize any of the crops, but I have to make myself not sink my hands into the dark dirt. I could almost close my eyes and think I was home.

"Can I ever go home?"

"I knew this question was going to come up, and to be honest, Luna, I'm not sure you're ready for my answer. I have pondered on whether I should tell you, or if it would be easier from one of the other females to explain."

"You have all this technology, surely the monsters that stole us were not smarter than all of this." I hold my arms out pointing around at everything. *"I had a family, people I loved, dreams!"*

I watch him look away, what looks like pain crosses his features. He is struggling to ask me something. "Did you have a mate… on Earth?"

I stand here for a second, it takes a moment for my mind to comprehend what he is asking. *"No, none I remember anyway."*

He smiles and I can see the relief on his face. "Thank you for not breaking my heart. Unfortunately, the news I have to tell you will not be as kind. The sad part is and I hate to say this, but at one point, the Korgons who took you had better ships than we did, but this isn't something we should be talking about right now. Luna, honey, you have only been awake a short time…"

"Tordan, don't baby me. I have experienced more than most, and I know still less than some…but I refuse to put my head in the dirt and act like it's all going to be rainbows and roses from this point on."

He just looks at me, I can see him struggling and this just makes it worse. "You, Kira, Brittany…and only the Lord of Light knows how many more… were taken at the same time. All of you were abducted from different locations on your planet, but you were all stored on the same ship. That ship took between eighty and one hundred of your Earth years to reach…well here. So, by the time you were to be sold you had already been away from Earth…"

"Are you saying I was like, frozen, asleep, or practically dead for almost a hundred years? While those blue bastards floated this way?"

"I told you this would not be easy to hear."

I stomp off, throwing my hands into the air. *"Son, of a bitch… my whole fucking family is dead. I can't even imagine what my parents went through afterward. Hell's fire, Dad would have been lucky for them not to put him in a nuthouse. Because I can guarantee you this may be normal out here, but four-armed blue aliens are not a regular on Earth."*

I swear if I had the ability to scream right now, I would. I turn back towards Tordan only to watch him trying to hide a smile.

"You have the balls to laugh at me right now?"

"Oh, Luna honey, I'm not laughing at you or the circumstances… but I will say, I'm enjoying a side of you I didn't know existed. You have hidden this fire inside of you well."

I lean back against one of the beds, lifting my head up to look at the stars above and ponder how many times mom and dad wondered if I was alive out there. I'm glad they didn't know what truly happened to me.

"SAGE said something earlier and it didn't make any sense, she said she tried to research what I may have looked like but couldn't find anything. If you guys have no contact with Earth, how did she have that?"

"We only have limited information about Earth and its inhabitants. That's a huge story within itself."

"Can't you just send a ship or satellite or something there?"

"We did, and RaZ barely made it back, you see… Lord of Light, how do I explain this without getting into all the details?" He runs his hand through his hair looking up at the stars. "Ok, There was an epic collision with one of the larger planets in your solar system. When this happened, it knocked all the other planets off their original axis and your Earth exploded afterward. We have no knowledge of survivors. As of right now… as far as we know, there is just a small number of you left."

I slide down to the floor and pull my knees up to my chest, running the words he just said to me over and over. Tordan comes over and sits next to me. He doesn't touch me, but I can feel the warmth of his body next to mine.

"I'm sorry, Luna. I feel like nothing I have to say is good. I didn't plan on this rising going like this. I was hoping to give you every reason to laugh, instead, all I have done is diminish the fire inside of you."

I raise my head up and smile when I realize, even sitting on the floor, he is so much larger than I am that I'm looking at his chest. *"Tordan, did you take me away from my family? Did you abuse me? Did you destroy Earth? No, you didn't… if anything. You are trying to put all the pieces of me back together. I don't blame you…now don't get me wrong, I really want to blame something, but you're not it.*

"I can't believe our entire world is gone, maybe it will hit me harder later... but it's been gone for me for quite some time now. It's so sad though, I mean our histories, our cultures, knowledge...everything...just gone. I can remember working the fields on a hot summer day thinking how primitive the process was. Now we will never eat that fresh corn or have a mess of beans. There will be no stealing a tomato off the vine and sneaking out with a salt shaker late at night for a snack.

"One thing that never changes no matter where or how...is the struggle of adjusting to this nonstop thing called life."

Tordan takes my hand, pulling it to his lips kissing it gently. He doesn't push me to get up or even talk anymore, we just sit there. I don't know how long we have been there when I start hearing what sounds like little feet skipping our way.

"Unka Tordy, where you hiding? Falcor told me you were in here."

A huge smile appears on his face as he stands up. "I'm right here, Munchkin."

"Whatcha doin on the floor? No wonder I couldn't find you. You too big to play on the floor. Have you seen Danny?"

"You can't find the boy?"

"I wouldn't have asked you where he was if I could."

The little green bundle of energy looks over at me. "Oh, hi again... that is a really pretty dress you have on. Did CIP make it for you?"

I nod yes.

"Keida, Luna can't talk really well yet…her voice box has to wake up."

"Is it because she was asleep for so long?"

"Partially, yes. Now when was the last time you saw the boy?"

"I don't know, maybe this morning…but I started missing him, and then I couldn't find him anywhere. Then Mamaw said she was going to fix cookies and I knew he wouldn't want to miss those. So, I went to our room, and he wasn't there, then I went to our playroom thinking he was playing with that silly sword, but he wasn't there either. I started to tell Daddy I couldn't find him, but he was talking to Unka SoL. Then Papaw was talking to a counselor person…so I came to find you."

I can tell he is torn. *"Go on, I would head back to your room, but I know I would never find it on my own."*

"Munchkin, would you care to walk Luna back to my quarters?"

"How about I take her to meet Mommy first?"

He looks over at me and I shrug; as much as I would like to hide, that has never solved anything. I'm going to have to meet them all sooner or later. Might as well rip that band-aid off and just do it. As beautifully different as the little girl here is, I can't even imagine what her mother looks like. I need to have my game face on in case she has an arm growing out of her head or something.

"You, don't mind? You don't have to go, Luna…if you're tired she will take you back to our quarters."

"Our quarters?"

"You're mine, Luna. I know I will have to work for your affection, but in my mind, it's a done deal, until you tell me otherwise. I'm too old to play games. In that same sense age has taught me to not hesitate and take what you want or need. The moment I laid eyes on you I knew you were the one for me."

I'm not sure how to answer that so instead I change the subject, *"I'll go with the child. Is there anything I should know in advance?"*

"No, you are safer actually with the others than you are anywhere else."

"Unka Tordy, are you talking to her in your head like you do Papaw and Falcor? Because she ain't talking back."

"Yes, actually I am."

"That's soooo cool. One of these days I gotta get one of those."

She takes my hand in hers and starts pulling me back the way she just came. "Come on, we will go this way, I'll show you my favorite flower. It's over here. Unka Tordy, when you find Danny you tell him he is so grounded."

I smile back at Tordan as she leads me forward sending him a small wave just as I lose sight of him.

CHAPTER 30

TORDAN

"Falcor, I'm going to assume you had a good reason not to inform Keida of Danny's whereabouts."

"Affirmative, sir."

"Where is he?"

"He is currently in a private simulator room I have conducted for him next to our primary energy core."

"What! No one but authorized personnel should be on that level."

"If you would proceed that way, I have also notified Commander SoL, Commander DaR, and General XuL to meet you there. I have once again overstepped my programming. The male was in need of instant relief. Before he hurt himself or someone else, and this was the best course of action."

I round the corner only to run into DaR. "And here I thought it was only the females we were going to have to worry about."

"I didn't know the boy had any issues."

"I think we are simply used to the oddness of everyone and didn't think this was any different. How is your female?"

"She is adjusting… better than I thought she would actually. She is with Keida right now. Our little Munchkin has grown a foot since I have been gone."

"That youngling is going to be a heartbreaker. She grows more beautiful every rising."

We are almost to the main reactor when the wall opens up, showing us that XuL and SoL are already inside, looking through a two-way wall monitor.

SoL's massive arms are crossed as he watches the young human male throw what looks like balls of energy at the wall.

"Falcor, now that we're all present, report," he barks out.

"Danny started to build up large quantities of energy right after he captured and held the imposter, SiN. I don't know where his powers originate from, but the hound he calls Raven also displays these same traits.

"It appears that when angered, or in states of high emotion, he has a hard time containing the energy pulsing under his skin. I have witnessed the color of his eyes changing multiple times and simply assumed because none of the females seemed to be concerned that this was something natural for their human species.

"I have researched every record available and can find no reference or reasoning behind it. I found him this rising hiding in a closet, he was taking huge breaths trying to calm his breathing down. I watched him pile clothes over his head when he heard Keida calling out his name and I thought that was out of character for him because they are inseparable. So, I decided against my programming to approach the youngling.

"He was scared to be around everyone because he said he can't get the light to stop. I had him touch the wall inside the closet and I will be truthful here, he is packing quite the punch in that small frame of his.

"I brought him here and created a safety wall around the perimeter so that no one could enter until he felt like he was back under control. My main power core is close enough to simply absorb the energy he is conducting, and no one is at risk of being harmed.

"The hound Raven also puts off this same energy, except she slowly dissipates in through the ground when she walks. The first time she walked through my hallway I could feel little charges with every step. The only comparison I can provide is to being stung. I believe Danny was also distributing his power the same way, and it's only because they have been on the ship for quite some time now that his body had a huge reserve of excess."

SoL's voice rings out through the room, "How did this youngling hold SiN when none of the rest of us could?"

"Somehow, he is pulling together air molecules, and they are being charged so quickly it's like he is making a lightning storm within himself. He simply projected it outwards. In other words, he basically trapped the dark mist that makes up SiN and held it until he was ready to either tear him apart or release the energy."

I wasn't shocked that this was XuL's question. "Is the boy safe to have around Keida or the others?"

"Yes, General… He is well aware of what is coursing through him. He simply didn't have the means or the know-how to get any relief from it. Apparently, the only calmness he gets is with Keida. That's why he cannot sleep if not next to her, she is the only thing that regulates or even dissipates the power inside of him. My personal belief on this is as to why,… is Mistress Keida's genetics were formed in the purity pools. Her very core is calm, and healing."

DaR smacks the glass in front of him. "If that is the case, why was he hiding? Why not bring this problem to one of us instead of concealing it?"

"He is young, Commander and is still learning. I believe the male needs to be trained not only physically, but mentally. He is small for his kind and even though the power inside of him could easily destroy an enemy, he doesn't have enough control of it right now to use it effectively. The male was merely lucky with SiN. He needs to build his physical strength to offset the interior."

"I am impressed that you even took it upon yourself to help the boy, Falcor. I take it you have a plan in place."

"Yes, General Tordan, I do… I believe Commander DaR has already started his physical training. I think it would be in the male's best interest to continue this and then I can personally work with the other. I will speak to SAGE about building a safe room for him planetside."

I watch the boy twirl his wrist casually as a ball of light grows in his small frame. His eyes swirl an eerie bright blue, if you look closely it's like he is sitting inside a bigger form of himself, or something else. He is outlined in an aura I have never witnessed before.

"I'm going to speak to Tyberius in depth about how the boy came to be on the ship with them. I believe there had to be some sort of occurrence on Earth that caused this molecular change within him. Until then, I will put precautions in place."

"Thank you, Falcor, for taking immediate action. I have been skirting my duties and should have caught this, but I have been preoccupied with the circumstances of Targres Four and Luna. Commander SoL, I should have informed you that I'm not sure at this point when I will return to full duty."

"Tordan, there are plenty of us on board. Enjoy winning over your little human, because if she is anything like my Alana,… she is well worth the effort. Falcor, we give you full permission to proceed further. Gentlemen, as Alana would say, I'm ready for substance and the company of my female."

"I believe Keida said they were all together in the main lounge."

"Then we have a destination, age before beauty... Father, you and Tordan lead on."

I look over at DaR as we start walking out of the room. "If he wasn't so damn big, DaR, I think we could take him."

I don't know who is laughing more when suddenly SoL throws me and DaR over his shoulders, packing us both down the hall like we are younglings. Our laughter can be heard throughout the ship.

CHAPTER 31

LUNA

This child is so full of energy and life you can't help but smile around her. The way she talks and forms her words shows that she has to have some humans around her or else she wouldn't put some of the slang together the way she does.

We no longer leave the room with all of the plants than a large steel-like door opens. We walk through it only for a set of red lights to scan us from top to bottom. I start to pull her back from the lights.

"It's ok, …it's just Falcor, he is just scanning us to make sure we don't have any bugs on us. They got all kinds of crawlies in the dirt back there."

I can hear the sound of voices before I see them. There is a group of girls standing in front of a large table of some sort.

Keida lets go of my hand, running forward only to grab some-one's legs from behind, hugging them tightly.

"Mamaw, are they done yet? I brought Tordan's girl with me too."

They all turn towards me at once. The one Keida had just hugged is stunning. Long dark blond hair hangs in a thick braid all the way past her butt. She puts you in the mind of a young Catherine Seymore, her features are so naturally luminesced she is practically perfect. Another bends down, picking Keida up, placing her on her hip. She is young, possibly just out of high school with long, wavy auburn hair that she has casually thrown over one shoulder. Her eyes are so dark they are practically pierc-ing, there are black tattoos on her skin…and I swear, they look like they're moving around. I almost miss the third one, she is a tiny little thing. Her coloring is so different from the others, she is ghostly pale, with large blue eyes, but it's her hair… it's so light it's almost colorless, and it appears to have small rods woven throughout it.

I immediately feel ugly compared to their immense beauty. The first one is definitely human, but the others…they seem more. They are still very much human but altered somehow.

"You're awake, it's such a pleasure to finally meet you. Tordan wouldn't allow us to come to your rooms yesterday, he is so over-protective. SAGE was just telling us that she was making you some more clothes and that you seemed to be doing well.

"I'm sorry, here I'm already overwhelming you, let me introduce myself. I'm Kira, and that's Brittany, you have already met our little bundle of joy Keida, and the one we were just teasing about getting a booster seat for is Alana."

I smile and nod my head toward them all. "Hi," I barely get out.

"Oh, she can't talk, Mamaw. Her voice is sleeping or something, Unka Tordan said."

"My goodness, that has to be troubling, well don't worry about it, we will talk your head off, you probably couldn't have gotten a word in anyway. Would you like something to drink? I just fixed some iced tea, and yes, I have finally managed to get it to taste just like home."

I smile and shake my head, yes, hoping I can at least find my mouth this time to take a drink on my own. Conversations carry on all around me. I smile when I feel like I should, but for the most part, I simply enjoy being a part of something so special.

I didn't do a very good job of hiding the shock of finding out that Brittany is Keida's mother. At no point did I think the child's mother was human. I simply assumed she belonged to an alien couple who worked or lived on Falcor.

We all sat down on a set of huge couches sipping tea when I notice they all have matching marks on their arms. Kira is sitting closest to me, and without thinking I touch her arm gently pointing at the mark. Then point to all the other girls, it is getting frustrating not being able to ask them the things that were going through my head. I managed to say, "Same." Then,… "The…same…?"

"Are you sure you want to talk about all this?"

I shake my head yes, I'm tired of not knowing…even if I don't like the answer.

She reaches, turning my wrist over and then frowns. "I don't know why Tordan didn't do this while you were under. He knows the danger you are in by not being marked."

I pull back away from her. She can tell she has alarmed me. "Damnit, Kira that sure as shit came out wrong."

"Mom, you said a bad word."

"Sorry baby. Luna, what Kira is trying to say… is not to worry, you will have one the same as ours. More than likely before you leave this room, and no, it does not hurt."

Keida jumps off Brittany's lap and comes over to sit by me. She grabs my hand in her small one and I smile sadly down at her. Hopefully, she can see how much I appreciate her kindness. Then I point to the marking that is even on Keida's arm.

"This mark you see on all of us is called a house mark, the House of DaR exactly. This mark shows the outside world that you are under the protection of this particular house. And until we arrived," she points to the girls around me, "only DaR, Tordan, and his sons had this mark."

"Kira, quit beating around the bush and just tell her."

She takes my other hand and looks down. I can immediately tell this is not something she likes to talk about. "I had just woken up in what I thought was a coffin at the time. There was a weird voice echoing throughout the house and my whole world had been destroyed. I had no idea who was the good guy or the bad, but my first instinct was to run. I knew better, but I ran anyway. I found myself in a huge market, surrounded by things...no human mind can fathom. I hadn't walked more than a few feet into the crowd when something grabbed my arm. In my ignorance, I had convinced myself I would find a ship and go home.

"Anyway, Lord, I remember looking up and swearing I was staring at Satan himself. The male who grabbed me was an easy six-and-a-half foot tall, absolutely huge, and blood red. He had black markings all over his body and face, but it was the horns that were the most terrifying. He put you in the mind of the devil in the movie *Legend* if you ever saw it.

"He had a couple of friends with him and at first he was just studying the new alien in front of him. Until he turned my wrist over and saw that I was not marked. He started dragging me off and told me if my master was too stupid to mark me then he would take me for himself. I fought with everything I had. I knew if I got on that ship with him, the torture I had already gone through would feel...well, I knew it was going to be bad.

"Then something roared, unlike anything I had ever heard before. DaR came through that crowd, and I swear it was like Mosses splitting the red sea. The creature who grabbed me was called a Phogx and he was just as determined to keep me as DaR was to save me. DaR cut him and the two others down, unlike anything I had ever seen before. To say the least… I never ran again. It wasn't hard to figure out who the good guys were after that.

"So, as you can see, the mark is important. Especially for us… it gives us a freedom we would never have any other way. Because no one wants to be on DaR's bad side."

"I'm glad that I'm good for something, my Kira."

The sound of an odd male's voice has me jerking to my feet. I grab Keida, pulling her close to me and start backing up as three huge things walk in the door. Keida breaks out of my hold, running right up to the fierce, but harsh-looking green one, yelling, "Daddy."

He picks her up, kissing her on the cheek and even though his markings are terrifying you can tell he adores the child. I can see immediately how much she favors him. But I am still shocked when he goes over and kisses Brittany before he settles down on the couch with Keida on his lap.

Then suddenly the room gets really small. I don't realize I am still slowly walking backward until I hit the wall behind me. My mind can almost not comprehend the mass of the solid gray… thing coming through the doorway next. He is so large he has to duck down to get his horns through and his skin looks almost like concrete.

He takes two steps, picks tiny little Alana up, and sits her on his lap, his horns immediately intertwining with her hair. Hair that I thought had rods in it. She looks like a kid sitting on a giant's lap.

And I will say that I'm ashamed of the fact that the tall cool drink of water that walked in next practically takes my breath away. Even being an alien, he was a beautiful specimen of a male, and I'm not shocked in the slightest that he is the one Kira has been talking about… this is the famous DaR.

I practically jump out of my skin when someone touches my arm and the second I see it's Tordan, tears fill my eyes. I have no idea where he comes from, but I don't think I have ever been this happy to see anyone…ever. It's like in my mind his very presence means safety. Tordan pulls me close; he must have been able to tell how overwhelming all this is for me.

Brittany doesn't waste a second. "Tordan, are you going to explain to us why Luna isn't marked?"

I see him turn my arm over and frown. Then the holographic appears on the table in the middle of the room.

"Brit, quit giving Tordan a hard time. He put in for the mark to be applied, but I had to make sure her skin grafted perfectly to her hand first. I had spent rotations freeing her skin of scars and I refused for this mark to hinder that process. I have her scheduled for it to be applied in two risings."

A squeaky laugh leaves my throat when the hologram crosses her arms and starts tapping her foot, looking at Brit.

"Sorry, Tordan. SAGE, you could have just told us this when this conversation started."

"I was busy elsewhere. I have an entire wardrobe to oversee, dwellings planetside to run; I'm busy. I would have been here sooner but I informed the cooks that you will be eating in your private quarters this darkness. So, you all can stay here and relax, it will be presented momentarily. Ladies, did you tell Mistress Luna how beautiful her reconstruction was and that you recognized her?"

I see Kira and Brit glance over at each other before they both look away. I have no idea what SAGE is talking about. I have never seen either of these women before in my life.

I glance over at Tordan, he is practically gritting his teeth. I can tell he is trying not to say anything.

"What…I dnt?" God, I hate not being able to talk.

Brittany shakes her head. "SAGE, as much as I love you, sometimes I wish I could strangle that little neck of yours."

"I don't understand the sudden tension in the room. I have rewound my words and see no fault in them."

I watch Kira start twisting her hands together, and I'm not shocked to see Keida crawl up in her lap, wrapping her little arms around her neck as DaR sits them both on his lap.

"Ho..w?" I keep trying to ask them.

Kira's voice is so soft at first that I almost can't hear her. "Luna, I don't know if you are aware that Brittany and I were both taken at the same time as you were. We were also awakened at the same time on the way to Sybrus One… which we found out later was nothing more than a slave auction planet. Brit and I recognized you the other day in the med chamber; you see, we were in the same area you were. You were already in the room when they brought us in…throwing us on the tables. We…watched first-hand…what they did to you. I was convinced you were dead … when they took you away. How you are sitting here in front of us today is a miracle and a dedication to the strength inside of you. You were so strong, you never stopped fighting them. I didn't have your strength or willpower to fight back."

"You..urt…bad..too?"

She shakes her head yes. Tears form in Kira's eyes and Keida wipes a stray one off her cheek.

"Don't cry Mamaw, Papaw made all the bad men go away."

"I know, baby, but sometimes bad memories still hurt…even if it's been a long time."

Tordan kisses the top of my head. I can feel myself start to tremble all over. My mind flashes back to that day. I remember so vividly it's like I'm still there. They just kept bringing girl after girl into that room. I can hear the laughter of the monsters around us. The screams, the smells. I don't know if I made a noise or what, but the next thing I know Tordan is laying me down on a bed.

He pulls the covers up over me and I wrap them up in my fist tightly, turning on my side. The bed tilts a little and I feel him lie down before he pulls me close, spooning in behind me.

"Try to sleep Luna, you have had a very trying day."

CHAPTER 32

LUNA

I open my eyes, suddenly awake. I don't know if I slept any, but my mind isn't flashing now like a camera roll. I lay here curled up against Tordan, enjoying his soothing warm presence behind me. *Damn, this whole situation is so fucked up.* I must have projected that rather loudly, because he pulls me closer, and when he kisses my neck, a small shiver flows down my arms.

"You didn't sleep long."

I don't turn toward him. I just lay there looking at the wall. I feel him reach above his head, and before my eyes, the whole wall disappears in front of me. It's like I'm lying in a bubble surrounded by stars.

"I had Falcor install this rotations ago. I have a hard time quieting my mind sometimes and I find the quietness of space soothing."

"My mother was a huge stargazer. I don't think Dad enjoyed it the way she did, but he never complained when she wanted to stay up late to watch a meteor storm, or just stare up at the sky. It is quite beautiful, isn't it?

"I was just thinking about some of the things Kira said. It makes me wonder how many other girls are out there. As bad as I hate to think about it, there were dozens of girls in that room…so many lives were destroyed and changed forever. So many families left behind, always wondering what happened to their loved ones.

"The guy she was talking about that grabbed her in the market was Hugo, wasn't it?"

"Yeah, you could say… I was shocked to see him alive in that compound with you."

"He was always so kind to me. I would never have pictured him being who she explained. At least now some of the things you guys said to each other makes more sense. Did DaR recognize him also?"

"Oh, yeah…I had to remind him twice that he had already terminated his life once and that he had done nothing to deserve it a second time. EvO is planetside with him right now. That's one of DaR's twenty-two…well, twenty-three sons. He is helping rebuild the compound and scientific sector of the planet."

"What? Twenty-plus?"

"That's a story for another day. Anyway, I'm hoping DaR can get past the mistakes the big Phogx made and be able to help him with reinstatement into society. He will never be able to go back to his people, but that doesn't mean he can't have a full life on Targres Four. We could use a few more allies on that planet.

"I wasn't going to ask you this, but I feel like you should know it's an option. Do…or would you like to have your memories dampened? I hate watching you relive those horrors over and over."

I turn towards him quickly. *"Are you for real? You leave my damn head alone. Lord knows as screwed up the last years have been,… I still wouldn't wish any of it on my worst enemy. But it happened to me, and I have every right to be sad, pissed, or happy about it. You keep your mind numb to yourself. I was a walking zombie long enough."*

He smiles and pulls me into his chest. "All that fire in such a little frame," he whispers.

The fight seems to just evaporate out of me. I know my emotions are all over the place. *"Tordan, why do you want me?"*

"Isn't that the magical question everyone asks at one time or another? What is it about that one person that draws them in? What is it that makes you believe you can't live through another rising without them in your arms? Is it the smile they bring to your face, or maybe it's the comfort of their company? Is it the way they fit against you, possibly the smell of their hair, or the way they look at you when they think you're not looking? I believe we all have that person who is our negative or positive when needed. I also think some people simply fit together like a piece of a puzzle. So, to answer all of this, you are and were the missing piece of my puzzle. I have looked for you my whole life, you simply fit…and I couldn't be happier to be here,… right here and now with you. Now go to sleep, the world can wait."

CHAPTER 33

LUNA

Tordan snores lightly behind me and even though it takes some wiggling, I finally free myself of his large frame to go to the bathroom.

SAGE appears on the counter as I'm trying to figure out how to brush my teeth. "Mistress Luna, I apologize if anything I said last rising upset you. Your happiness is my first priority; it causes me great distress if I believe I have failed at that."

"No SAGE, you simply made everyone quit walking on eggshells around me. If I have a problem with you, I promise, you will be the first to know."

"How is the throat this morning? Would you like to refresh yourself in the Ionizer or a bath?"

"My throat is sore but tolerable. And I have had enough vapor-like showers to last me a lifetime. I can see where if you are in a hurry they would be wonderful, but if I'm not on a schedule, I want a bath."

"I will prepare it for you, while the water is filling the tub I would love to show you something." The wall to the closet opens and it's like I have never been in this room before. The closet is huge, there are rows of different kinds of shoes and a dressing table. Ceiling-to-floor mirrors all around, and even what looks like a washstand at a hair salon in one corner. "What do you think?"

"Wow, it looks like something you would see in a magazine."

A section of a wall moves outwards and a rack emerges, lined with clothes. It turns slowly, showing me that everything is color-coordinated. "These are all yours, and they should fit accordingly."

"SAGE, I couldn't wear all of these in a lifetime, but thank you…I'm over-whelmed by your thoughtfulness."

"Oh, this is just the beginning, your closet is still rather small compared to Mistress Kira's. Come, your bath is ready."

I pull yesterday's clothes off that I slept in and sink down into the water, making myself close my eyes as I blank every thought out of my head. But the sudden feeling of being watched has me opening my eyes only to see Tordan standing over me. The pair of loose pants he has on accentuates the V of his waistline and the huge erection he has. My first reaction is to cover myself, but then I remember the pleasure I felt in his arms. Being in his arms is the only place everything stops.

"Can I join you?" He motions for me to scoot forward. As I lean up, the tub itself starts to change shape. I practically crawl over the side when it starts to enlarge. Tordan puts his hand on my shoulder. "Relax, Falcor is just rearranging the tub so that I don't smash you."

"Relax my ass, dammit. Tordan, this is not normal. I swear, will I ever quit being surprised, or scared out of my wits? Do you know what's normal? Your big ass would barely be able to squeeze in here with me, and we would be all smashed together. Water would slosh over the sides and then we would probably end up having some sort of water fight or fighting over the washrag. Now, you're going to have your own dance space in this expanding tub, and I'm going to have to come up with a smooth move to crawl all over you. I didn't even get to see you undress because I was over here trying to not be eaten by the alien tub."

His laughter is like a balm to my soul. He grabs me around the waist tucking me in between his legs as he leans my head back against his chest. "Luna, I don't believe I have laughed so much…well, ever to be honest. You are good for the soul, and you don't have to have any reason to crawl on me as you put it. I'm easily available when it comes to you. Here give me that sponge and let's see how much exploring I'm allowed to do."

I reach over only to take the sponge for myself. I soap it down and pull his leg up, bending it at the knee beside me. Then run my hands down his long leg from the inside of his thigh all the way to his huge foot. When I start my way back up the other side, I turn in his arms, straddling his legs. Pulling back just enough that I'm sitting on his thighs. He lets go and puts his arms out on both sides of the tub, but never takes his eyes off me. He moans when I run the sponge across his chest and waist. I trace the muscles lightly fascinated by their reaction from the slight brush of my hand. I lean forward still not touching the one place I know he is aching the most and nip at his nipples only to feel his shaft jerk against my stomach.

"You know two of us can play this game, little one."

I smile back at him and pull myself flush against his chest, trapping his hardened length between us. He grabs my hips under the water and grinds himself against me. Then reaches up gripping my head, his finger sliding through the curls on my head. I get nervous when I realize what he is planning on doing.

"Your hair feels like twirled silk underneath my fingers," he whispers, a breath away from my lips.

I haven't been kissed or even able to kiss in so long. It will be like my first time all over again. He nibbles at my bottom lip and I relax in his arms. It takes me a few tries, but finally, I feel my lips moving against his, learning the things that make him grip me tighter. A moan leaves my throat as I reach between us taking him in hand stroking his complete length up and down slowly. Even though I know he has been inside me already, I'm shocked that he fits. I take my time, learning the things that make him squirm as I rub along the bumps and ridges lining his alien shaft.

Tordan bites and nibbles his way down my chest as I rise up out of the water craving more of what he is giving me. Impatiently, I grab his shaft rubbing it against my inner folds. My body is wet and aching, I don't give him the chance to stop me or change positions as I lower myself upon him. I have to rise up several times as my body adjusts to his size. Then I slowly start grinding myself up and down as he thrusts upwards. His hands and mouth are all over me. My body becomes putty in his large hands as the intensity of all of this overwhelms me.

I can hear the water hitting the floor as I seek my own release. Tordan kisses me breathlessly, his tongue mimicking the things our bodies are doing together. I cling to his strength as he thrusts hard into me and with a single flick of his finger, my body soars. Just a few thrusts later, I feel Tordan's body tense up under me and the hot feeling of his release inside of me.

I lay against his chest, both of us breathing hard as he rubs my back. I have no idea how long I lay in the water against him, simply relaxed, but I whine when he pulls out of me.

"One of these days we are going to do that on a bed, so I can worship you properly, but I will never look at a bath the same way again. As much as I hate to get up, we need food, and I want to show you something."

"Do we have to? I really like it here. You are so damn comfortable." I squeak when he smacks my ass and water goes everywhere.

"Comfortable. Just for that, I should make you wait for your surprise."

I stick my lips out, pouting. Then smile when I realize I can pout again. Tordan runs his fingers over my lips. "Would you look at the beauty of that smile. Luna, honey…you take my breath away." He kisses me softly once again before he lifts both of us out of the water effortlessly. I will say I love the way he packs me around.

A couple of towels appear in the magic drawer again, and I dry off with one, then start to use the other one to get the water off of the floor.

"You don't have to do that. Honey, Falcor has mini drains on the floor that you can't see. He will pull all the water back to the main tanks and retreat it. Go get dressed in that fancy room you have now, and I'll wait out in the bedroom for you."

SAGE meets me the moment the wall opens. "Let's see what we can clothe you with this rising. I think I may have the perfect thing." Moments later, I'm dressed in a loose pair of pants with a matching shirt that ends right above my waistline that shows a teasing amount of skin on my stomach. I keep pulling the shoulder up but then SAGE shows me it's supposed to be worn down on one side. I slip on cute matching shoes. A quick tease to my damp curls, and I start out of the room.

Feeling light-hearted and like a girl for the first time in a long time, I walk into the bedroom, hating the fact that Tordan is completely covered in his normal uniform. I twirl around. *"What do you think?"*

"I think that if I didn't want to give you this surprise so badly, I would like nothing better than to strip you out of that and mate with you the rest of the rising. But you look stunning. Come here... I had forgotten I had this until now."

I watch him raise up his cybernetic arm and a small drawer emerges from its side. He motions for me to turn around. "SAGE, can you put one of the portable viewers in front of Luna please?"

A small mirror appears in front of us and this is the first time I have seen us like this. His huge gray frame completely engulfs mine as he has what feels like a foot of girth all around me. His large hands look way too big to handle the delicate item he is placing around my neck.

I feel my whole body simply stop. I don't think I even take a breath when he moves his hands away... He watches my emotions in the mirror.

My hand reaches up and I rub the familiar necklace. The gold heart hangs on a long rope chain... lined with diamonds twirling around one side. My dad gave me this when I was a little girl, and I never took it off. I hadn't thought about it in years, I just assumed it was lost.

"How...where?" I squeak out.

"That first day in the market, I saw you stop and look at it. I had a feeling it was more than just a simple piece of jewelry to you. I almost got shot getting it, but I wasn't leaving without it."

I turn around and launch myself into his arms, wrapping my legs around his huge frame. *"Tordan, you have done so much for me. I can never thank you enough, for this gift…this new body, and another chance at happiness."*

"Honey, I would give you the whole universe if this is always your response."

"Thank you for this surprise."

"Oh, that isn't the surprise. I plan on getting a few more of these hugs before this rising is over." He lowers me back to the floor and tries to pull my shirt down when he sees my skin showing.

"Do you not like it? I can go change."

"No, at first I was just trying to figure it out; women's clothing is complicated. Some things are up, others are down. You wear whatever you want or that is comfortable for you. I personally prefer you naked. So, clothes are now a personal enemy that is intent on hiding that lovely body of yours from me."

He pulls me out of the room and we head down the hall. He puts us in that tube thing again. "Falcor is always monitoring the lift tubes, just tell him where you want to go and he will take you to that level." We get off on the floor that has all the crops on it and I glance up at him, wondering if he forgot he had already shown me this. When the wall opens, I'm shocked at all the empty beds being prepared and the boxes sitting everywhere.

"When we came here last rising, one of the things you said to me was how sad you were that you would never be able to eat another tomato or a piece of corn. Now, I have no idea what those are besides what I have seen on the holo screens, but what I do have… are seeds.

"You see, when Tyberius returned to us from Earth, he brought boxes and boxes of seeds with him. He was a botanist on Earth and the very thought of all of those plants being lost forever made him sick. So, he knew he had four or five years to gather what he needed, and by the looks of all of this, I don't know how they got the shuttles off the ground. But because of his determination not only do we have soil samples, but we also have books on how to grow them. I wanted to give you a piece of home, something familiar as the girls call it.

"I also wanted to tell you that we can build a home anywhere you want. I will give up my position on Falcor, anything to keep that smile on your face and you in my arms. I was selfishly hoping that this would be a project you would love to oversee because I think you're the perfect person for it, but once again you don't have to. Where you go, so do I.

"So, surprise! …I hope… you're not jumping in my arms… Frack, and I was so sure you would love this."

"What I love is you! Do you have any idea what gift this is… not just to me, but for every human who lost their home?"

"You love me? So, this was a good surprise… then why are you not in my arms?"

I hold my arms up and he lifts me effortlessly, my arms circle his neck and my legs wrap around his waist.

"You know, even with all the heartache and the suffering, I would do it all again if I would have known this… You… were waiting right here for me. I love you, my big alien, and wherever you are is fine with me, you are my happy place."

He squeezes me tightly. "I love you my little human, and I will spend every moment and every breath showing you how much."

EPILOGUE

I have just gotten dressed when the door to our room suddenly opens and all the girls come flowing in.

Kira grabs me, hugging me tight. "I hope you didn't have plans because we have come to awaken that voice box of yours.

"You see, Alana, being our Alien language geek, was looking up how to get your voice box working and the crazy part is…it was so simple… It's singing. So, we decided to bring you a piece of home. ANDI, SAGE, Falcor… light it up.

The main room in our quarters starts changing. The couches are moved out of the way and a dance floor emerges in the middle of the floor. The girls start jumping up and down when the music comes on. I stand there laughing as I watch Keida twirl around and around in her skirt the two holograms dancing on the floor with her. All the girls are singing at the top of their lungs at a Pat Benatar song I loved as a teenager.

I have no idea when I started singing myself, but before long we were all shaking our asses and dancing around having the time of our lives. The door opens and I see the shock of what we are doing on Tordan's face.

I scream out, "Tordan, come dance with me," and the girls all cheer.

He grabs me, throwing me up in the air like you would a kid and I hear Keida yell, "Me next."

"You said my name!"

"I did, and boy are you in trouble now, you're going to wish for my silence before long."

"Tell me you love me!"

"I LOVE YOU"…… *and I really do*.

The End

Other books from this Author:

The Water Skippers series

Water Skippers

(Kyle and Eden)

A Dragonfly's Whisper

(Nora and Roman)

Earth Shadow

(Lorene and Garret) part one

Shadow Reborn

(Garret and Lorene)

Petal

(Randy and Petal)

Miranda and the Dragonfly King

(Miranda and Tagon)

Stand-alone novel
The Playboy and the Waitress

The Forsaken series
Forsaken
(Lucas and Emma)
Betrayed
(Tavish and Eve)
Forgotten
(Tyberius and Victoria)
Spin off to DaR

Darverius
DaR
(DaR and Kira)
XuL
(XuL and Brittany)
SoL
(SoL and Alana)
RaZ
(RaZ and Katherine)
A House of DaR Celebration (novella)
Tordan
(Tordan and Luna)

JENNIFER JULIE MILLER
WATER SKIPPERS SERIES
THE PLAYBOY
WATER SKIPPERS
DRAGONFLY'S WHISPER
EARTH SHADOW
SHADOW REBORN
PETAL
Miranda
Dragonfly King
THE PLAYBOY AND THE WAITRESS
THE FORGOTTEN SERIES
HOUSE OF DAR SERIES
FORSAKEN
BETRAYED
FORGOTTEN
DaR
SoL
RaZ

NOTE FROM THE AUTHOR

I hope… I have made you laugh, and possibly… even squeezed a few tears out of ya. Writing has been a lifelong dream for me, and our dreams are the only thing we have to build on!!!

So GO for it!!!!

I'm an avid reader myself. I believe there are Dragons, Unicorns, and multicolored Kitty Cats, because our imaginations are our own uniqueness.

I want to thank my family and friends for all your support.

To my readers, thank you for encouraging me to continue writing even though my worlds are little different.

After all, I'm Appalachian, and I talk Appalachian. Therefore, I write Appalachian. All my books have country girls in them, and that's mainly because I only know how to speak country girl correctly.

Then to the Lord above, whose blessing gave a poor little girl from Ironton a chance to dream!

If you enjoyed this story, or any of my other ones, I ask that you take a few minutes of your time, and leave a review on Amazon, or Goodreads. It really helps new and older authors alike.

If you would like to stay in touch, hear about new releases, give some advice, or just drop a line.

You can find me on Facebook.

Https://facebook.com/JenniferJulieMiller.

On Twitter.

Https://www.twitter.com/jenniferrick

Or email me at:

Jenniferjuliemiller@gmail.com

Follow me on bookbub. **Https://www.bookbub.com/pro-file/jennifer-julie-miller**

Follow me on Amazon.

Https://amazon.com/author/jjm5325903

And sign up for my email if you want to learn more about Darverius and DaR's twenty-two plus sons.

Http://eepurl.com/cfrL8X

DAR

Kira

In the blink of an eye, my whole world has collapsed around me. Headed towards my dream vacation I was snatched right out of the air. My husband, the love of my life, was destroyed right in front of my eyes. He fought bravely, trying to protect me from a horror neither one of us could have ever imagined. I find myself standing in the spotlight on a stage. Mutilated and tortured, the blood from my body flowing freely down my legs along with my will to live. Piercing yellow eyes emerge from the darkness, but even the shadows can't hide his imposing form. Gentle, but terrifying arms reach out for me and within their embrace can I find the will to live again?

DaR

I am a bad ass, known throughout the galaxy for my brutality, as a ruthless and feared commander. With that being said, somehow, I still got coerced into purchasing a slave. My eyes fall upon a small female whose very essence and eternal light is leaking out of her onto the floor below her. I watch in awe as she accepts her fate, willing her nightmare to be over. I almost turn away from her and the unnecessary cruelly in this room, but the very thought of her dying on that floor surrounded by the very monsters that have done this to her disgust me. I walk up among the beings surrounding her and pull her from the stage, daring, or should I say hoping they try to do something about it. The moment I put her in my arms, everything changed. The attachments I have avoided my whole life become unavoidable. Will this damaged slave be able to replace the shadows in my life? One thing for sure is that I will destroy the entire universe to keep her safe. No one touches what's MINE!

XUL

Brittany

All my dreams and wants were stolen from me in the blink of an eye. Awakening, in the middle of a nightmare, I realize I'm being sold like an animal to be studied and dissected in the name of science. Then tragedy strikes, leaving me abandoned and sick. I am only moments from taking my last breath when strong arms pull me from the darkness. I thought it was a blessing that he had found me, the green man who had haunted my dreams. I let myself believe, for just one moment, I might find a small piece of happiness in this unknown world. But what is the old saying? *'Don't count your chickens until they hatch!'*

A blood sucking parasite is eating me alive, literally, and no matter what, I'm not going to survive this horror story. My body is failing me. I beg him to let me go; I just want the pain to stop, but he won't listen. He holds me down and I struggle weakly against his immense strength, choking as blood fills my lungs, when I can't fight any more, Death opens its arms and invites me in.

XuL

My harsh, brutal features have deterred all females no matter the species. I long for companionship and love. Then I find her, my Kismet, the only one made just for me. The one precious thing I would worship above all others. But the fates are cruel especially to a male like me.

I am being forced to destroy the fragile bond that has formed between us, as I have to make the hardest decision of my life. One that will make me lose her either way. I hold her small, struggling body against me, tears flow down my face as she begs me to stop. My heart is crushed as I watch the light leave her beautiful eyes. Upon her final breath, I vow not even Death will keep what's mine.

SOL

Alana

The question is, do I allow this dark moment in time to rob me of the life I could possibly have here? I have never known such horror or fear. If I hadn't experienced it myself, I would have never believed any other living thing could possibly do this to another. The scars may be gone on the outside now, but they will remain forever in my soul. They tell me I can never go back, all that I have ever known is gone. Where does this leave me in the world of monsters? He beckons me, promising me...the fairy-tale... the impossible dream. Everything I have ever wanted to hear! But I don't know if I'm strong enough to go forward as long as the shadows of our past pull me backwards.

SoL

I knew she was withholding the truth from me. I had no idea who I held in my arms, until it was almost too late. The moment her true essence was revealed to me, my body reacted, reaching out for the one thing I had been searching for my whole life... my Inamorata. The very mistress of my heart and now that I have finally found her. I will follow her through the sands of time... no matter how long it takes. I will find my way back to her... because she is MINE!

RAZ

Katherine

How do you go on when all of your wants and dreams have been destroyed? My loved ones were snatched right out of my hands, leaving me alone in a world of unknowns and terror. I'm lost in the in-between with no familiar paths to follow until the sound of a heartbeat and a whisper draws me back to the land of the living.

RaZ

The moment I laid eyes upon her face I knew there would be no distance I wouldn't travel to make her my own. Unknown forces try to steal her from my very arms and even if I have to fight the very essence of her world, the universe, or the very Gods we pray to. Nothing will stop me from making her MINE!

FORSAKEN

Lucas and Emma

Katherine's parents

The one question she often asks herself is *why*. Why has she never been enough? Why doesn't anyone truly want her? She was reminded daily that she was nothing but a worthless girl and only another mouth to feed. The last time she saw her family was the night they dumped her in a ditch on the side of the road and left her to die.

A kind woman took her out of that ditch and gave her a home. Her new family was every girl's dream until a single poisoned scratch took it all away. Emma was tossed away again, becoming a prisoner, and a slave to her circumstances. The one person the Cook enjoyed beating regularly. The day Cook sold her body, all of her hopes and dreams were destroyed. But one fateful night, after fighting for her life, she escapes this, Hell.

He finds her on the brink of death, naked, beaten, and barely alive. She thinks he is the Angel of Death, someone who will save her, but he is a real monster. Did she just trade one Hell for another? Will the memories he steals from her dreams soften his heart enough to make him care for something more than himself? Or will he turn her away, just to *Forsake* her, like all the rest?

Tavish and Eve

It seems the ones we love the most are the first to Betray us! One such Betrayal cost me everything: my home, my dreams, and almost my life. The second I started running, I knew I would never be who I was or may have wanted to be. All of my choices were taken away with two last breaths, hers and then my own.

The dreams of my youth were destroyed because of the selfishness of others. I fear my life will become nothing but a cold existence of shadows and detachment.

The poison consuming my very soul is nothing but an excuse for me to lash out at the unfairness of it all. It's exactly the justification I need to deliver the pain others have inflicted on me my entire life. Will the emotions of my untried youth destroy my future as I'm forced into a world I truly don't understand?

My own mind has become my worst enemy, and my fragile heart can't withstand another break. I know he's a deceiver, a devil in disguise sent to collect my grieving soul. He is the real monster my mother warned me about under the bed. If I let him, he will destroy me in the end with his mischievous smile and lying angel eyes.

To be loved is the only dream I have left, but we all know Betrayal is the one thing you can always count on to crush you.

FORGOTTEN

Tyberius and Victoria

(DaR's father)

I have known this evil was coming for me my whole life, but that doesn't mean I have looked forward to it! I have run from every sign of the darkness, even to the point of being invisible to the ones around me. I've spent my whole life lurking in the shadows of my family. Keeping myself separate from the ones I love, living my dreams, and wants through their eyes.

I had become so wrapped up in their worlds trying to ensure their happiness, that the day he appeared in front of me. I never once questioned what I was supposed to do. The one thing my family could always count on is that I'm loyal to fault. Even though I made sure never to get too attached because I was terrified the darkness would take them also, it will do anything it can to defeat me. My goal is to survive and to finally see the light.

I have prayed to every God, for this to pass me by, only to know they can't answer. This is my destiny. I will suffer agony unlike anything my mind can imagine, but to be worthy of the light. I need to find a way to face this darkness.

I will never show him an ounce of weakness, but I scream silently for help. I refuse to let him win because he wants me here for eternity. A soul withered in ice, and loneliness, Forgotten in this room of horrors.

All the stars line up for us one time or another. I just have to wait my turn.

THE PLAYBOY AND THE WAITRESS

Jenna

I was always told never to forget that I was worth something too! We all know that every little girl dreams of her knight in shining armor. A man who will ride up and save her from the evil things trying to destroy her. Then, of course, we all know they live happily ever after. My knight was untouchable... A Playboy, a man who stole my heart right out of my chest and with very little effort on his part. Unfortunately, he was also a man whose world I would never fit in. You can take the girl out of the country. You can dress her in nice clothes, have her smile beautifully as you parade her on your arm, but you never really take the country out of the girl. I reach out for the brightest of stars... only for him to leave my heart in pieces crumbling at my feet.

Dage

I watched her for weeks, every smile she bestowed on me captured me in a way no others had. Circumstances throw us together over and over and no matter how many times I hold her in my arms it's never enough. I didn't know what I was missing until she walked away. I know, I can't have them and her... so who will lose?